CHANGING PEOPLE'S LIVES
WHILE TRANSFORMING
YOUR OWN

CHANGING PEOPLE'S LIVES
WHILE TRANSFORMING YOUR OWN

Paths to Social Justice and Global Human Rights

JEFFREY A. KOTTLER
MIKE MARRINER

WILEY

John Wiley & Sons, Inc.

Published by John Wiley & Sons, Inc., Hoboken, New Jersey.

Published simultaneously in Canada.

Library of Congress Cataloging-in-Publication Data:

Kottler, Jeffrey A.
    Changing people's lives while transforming your own : paths to social justice and global human rights / by Jeffrey A. Kottler, Mike Marriner.
        p.   cm.
    Includes bibliographical references and index.
    ISBN 978-0-470-22750-3 (paper/dvd)
      1. Social justice.   2. Social action.   3. Social service.   4. Human rights.   I. Marriner, Mike.   II. Title.
HM671.K67   2009
303.3'7209—dc22
                                                                                    2008029092

Printed in the United States of America

10 9 8 7 6 5 4 3 2 1

Contents

Acknowledgments

Any project requires a degree of collaboration between many people in order to succeed. This book, based on our own work over the past decade, includes contributions from hundreds of students, faculty, and professionals who were willing to share their experiences. Lisa Gebo, our editor and friend at Wiley, has been instrumental in helping us make our vision a reality. Her encouragement, support, and passion for helping others have inspired us to tell our story with as much honesty and transparency as we can.

We are grateful for the assistance of Peggy Alexander, Marquita Flemming, and Sweta Gupta for their work helping to put the book into production.

Digumber Piya and Kiran Regmi are our partners in one project in Nepal. It was their vision that inspired us to devote such a significant part of our lives to helping neglected children.

All photographs in this book (except a few submitted by our interviewees) were taken by Jeffrey during his work on various projects around the world. The video footage on the accompanying DVD was also filmed by Jeffrey during his visits to Nepal. Mike produced and edited the film, as well as interviewed students and charitable visionaries around the globe. We both collaborated on the telling of these stories.

Preface

This book is a bit different than other textbooks you might have encountered in your classes. It tells the stories of a number of students, professionals, and faculty, in a variety of fields, who want to make a difference in the world beyond their own personal goals and ambitions. Although we introduce you to some of the basic concepts related to social justice, global human rights, service learning, community activism, and altruism, this book is intended as much to inspire as educate you. It presents the narratives of several individuals, not unlike you, who made choices—or, in some cases, just fell into situations—where they could be helpful to others in a significant way. Although many of these students majored in education, health, and human service fields, several others eventually ended up in engineering, business, the arts, and humanities. What they all have in common is their search for some way that they could be helpful to those who have been most neglected and marginalized.

OVERVIEW OF THE CONTENTS

The first part of the book introduces the case study of one project in Nepal that was launched by one of the authors (Jeffrey) to address issues of poverty, neglect, physical and emotional abuse, and the oppression of women and girls. Contained within this story are many of the elements that are often part of service learning, social justice, and charitable work—including the joys, satisfactions, frustrations, and crushing disappointments. In addition to describing the nature of the problems in South Asia that have led to gender and ethnic inequities, sex slavery, poverty, health crises, and civil war, we also tell the stories of many individuals who have joined us in our efforts, what they have gotten out of their experiences, as well as the realities of what led some of them to abandon their efforts. The stories we describe will introduce you not only to some amazing, unbelievable, gut-wrenching experiences, but also to some of the universal challenges that you might expect in your own efforts to help others. Also unique to this project is a description of the kind of reciprocal influence that takes place in helping efforts in which the participants were transformed almost as much as the people they were helping.

We tell the stories not only of our own efforts to make a difference, but also of inspiring figures who have launched their own projects or participated in those created by others. Many of the leaders and participants began their first efforts while in college, while others abandoned lucrative careers to renew their commitments to social justice issues. In most of the cases we profile, the projects began (or remain) modest efforts that are within the scope of almost anyone who has sufficient commitment and motivation.

Part II of the book tells the stories of a number of people—students, professionals, leaders of organizations—who describe what they do, how and why they do it, and what they get out of their efforts. These are not just optimistic tales with happy endings, but rather narratives that reflect the true realities of what it means to live and work under harsh conditions, dealing with the magnitude of problems that appear intractable, with crushing poverty, with corruption and violence, with social conditions that appear hopeless. Yet contained within these stories are the seeds of inspiration that may very well lead you toward your own path of making this world a better place.

Part III shares the stories of many social justice efforts from across the globe, individuals who are working to create a positive impact within their own defined niches. From individuals who have raised more than $25 million in microfinance funds and have been featured on *The Oprah Winfrey Show* to a 13-year-old boy who started a basketball "Shoot-a-Thon" to raise money for African children orphaned by AIDS, all of them share how they got to where they are today, as well as the lessons they've learned throughout the process. We make suggestions of ways to create the kind of adventures and experiences that are likely to be the most satisfying and transformative—for you as well as for those you help. It isn't necessary to take on some "big thing," or even to join a major organization or program; it is often the little things you do that can grow to become significant efforts in their own right.

This book is intended as a supplementary text for a variety of courses in the social sciences, social work, counseling, human services, education, nursing, family studies, pastoral studies, health, and other related professions. It can be used in a variety of introductory courses, at both the undergraduate and graduate level, to inspire students (and professionals) to connect with their deepest longings to help those who are most in need. This is a book of hope, of resilience, and of passionate and courageous efforts to change people's lives far beyond the narrow scope of your own community and immediate circle of influence.

IDEAS IN ACTION

Accompanying the book is a DVD that is intended to inspire you further through the stories of students, educators, and professionals who are featured in the text. You will see and hear team members struggle with various challenges along the way, as well as speak from their hearts about what they are experiencing. Regardless of their age or life experience, participants talk about the impact that being involved in a service project has had on their future goals and aspirations.

Each of three sections of the DVD consist of vignettes that show scenic footage, visits to villages, and interviews with those who participated in our project. You will join the team on their journey and then hear their reflections on what they learned and how they were transformed.

CHANGING PEOPLE'S LIVES
WHILE TRANSFORMING YOUR OWN

PART I

Birth of a Movement

CHAPTER 1

Paths to Social Justice

As North America and other Western countries become more culturally diverse, members of most professions are expected to develop greater sensitivity and responsiveness to persons of different backgrounds. Thus, one segment of college education in all majors and specialties is devoted to reducing *ethnocentrism*, that is, a limited view of the world based only on your own background. Depending on your race, ethnicity, religion, gender, geographic location, socioeconomic status, first language, age, sexual orientation, political convictions, and other such variables, you may perceive the world in ways that are quite at odds with those who have different experiences.

It may seem obvious that you can't learn greater cultural sensitivity by listening to a lecture or reading a book about the subject. Your experiences in this arena can best be enriched and expanded through some form of direct contact with other cultures and people of different backgrounds. That is one reason why college campuses work so hard to build a student body that represents as much diversity as possible. It is also why you are so passionately encouraged to educate yourself outside the classroom by becoming involved in some kind of cross-cultural experience. This could involve a semester abroad, an academic exchange, home-stays in different communities, participation in cultural events, service learning, or a volunteer project. In many of these options, the goal is twofold—you are furthering your own education at the same time you are helping to improve the plight of those less fortunate than yourself. Students who participate in such activities often report that they also develop skills that help them to be more collaborative, flexible, caring, and sensitive to those who are different from themselves (Boyle, Nackerud, & Kilpatrick, 1999).

ALTRUISM: DOING GOOD FOR OTHERS—AND YOURSELF

Why do people willingly give away part of their time, not to mention their money, resources, and energy, to help others who are less fortunate? Why would students select service majors or helping professions that often result in lower financial payoffs than their friends who choose business?

The simple answer, of course, is that we devote ourselves to the path that offers us the greatest personal satisfaction and meaning. For some, this can involve the accumulation of maximum wealth; for others it means making a constructive difference in the world—being useful to others in greatest need.

Helping Now, or in the Future

It's been, I don't know, four years, but seems like a lifetime since I've been in college. Graduation is coming, and believe me, I can't wait, but I'm also freaked out by it all. I've got so much debt I might have to rob a 7–11 store. Just kidding! Anyway, I figure it'll take me at least 10 years to pay off what I owe, and that's if I'm careful. I figure that I'll just find a really high-paying job, make a boatload of money, and then some-day I can contribute in an even bigger way later in life, like Oprah did or something. There is a part of me that really does want to go travel the world and try to help people who aren't as lucky as I am. I guess I could defer my loans for a few years, since there are programs out there that do that, but the debt would still be waiting for me when I returned. I may as well just get to work now. It sounds hopeless, but do I have another choice?

Altruism refers to behavior that is "other-focused." It represents benevolent, charitable actions that are not motivated by personal gain or the expectation of reciprocal favors (Post, 2007). This sort of selfless giving is done without major consideration as to how it will pay off in the future. Compare, for example, a student who volunteers to work for a public agency to beef up a resume to one who has no ulterior motive other than to be helpful. Consider the difference between someone who works for Make a Wish Foundation to help relieve the suffering of children versus one who thinks it will look good on graduate school applications. We are not saying that good and noble behavior cannot be combined with furthering one's own interests; we are suggesting that "pure" altruism has no personal agenda.

Regardless of whether you are interested in service to build your own career options or out of genuine interest in being useful to others, the effects can often be the same. When people are *really* honest with themselves, they will often admit that there are clear payoffs to them of a very personal nature.

- They feel like their lives are redeemed. They are doing something that seems like it matters.
- They are giving their lives greater meaning. Many have left high-paying jobs because they felt empty.
- They are paying back what others have given to them. They have been wounded or hurt earlier in life and recovered sufficiently to want to ease others suffering.
- They are following a spiritual path. This can be either self-serving (a ticket to heaven) or following divine inspiration.
- They are developing new areas of expertise and gaining valuable experience. This can range from beefing up one's resume to developing skills that will be useful in the future.
- They are hiding from things they wish to avoid. Helping others is a good distraction from dealing with issues that may be painful, or avoiding problems that feel overwhelming.
- They can feel like martyrs, making sacrifices and suffering deprivations for the greater good.
- They are feeling useful. Their sense of self-worth and importance can be directly related to the impact they believe they're having on others.

When Greg Mortenson was asked what motivated him to work so tirelessly building schools in remote areas of Central Asia, he didn't hesitate for a second: "The answer is simple: when I look in the eyes of the children in Pakistan and Afghanistan, I see the eyes of my own children full of wonder—and hope that we each do our part to leave them a legacy of peace instead

What I'm Meant to Do

School frustrates me. When I was a kid everyone said I had Attention Deficit Disorder, which I wish I did because then I would at least have an excuse. I just get so damn bored when I'm sitting in class! The idea of sitting in a desk job for the rest of my life scares the crap out of me. I need to find something active where I can be moving around all the time. Just because I'm not like everyone else doesn't mean I'm any less than them. And I do have a big urge to help others. I think a job in some kind of international aid work would be perfect for me. Sometimes I get worried that I'm not smart enough to help other people, but then I realize that I really can make a difference, even if I'm not a rocket scientist or something like that. I went to Africa last year on a weeklong trip to build schools, and it was amazing! I wasn't bored once, and I was really changing these people's lives! I know now that this is what I was meant to do. It may not be the most conventional path in life, but I love it and I'm going to go for it.

of the perpetual cycle of violence, war, terrorism, racism, exploitation, and bigotry that we have yet to conquer" (Mortenson & Relin, 2006, p. 335).

Many of these motives play a part in our own work, but the last one is especially relevant to Jeffrey's story.

FIXING A HAND

The old man stumbled down the rocky slope grimacing in pain. He was holding his arm, bent at the elbow, with his hand upright as if in a perpetual greeting. In spite of his advanced age, he seemed far more nimble on his feet than I (Jeffrey) could ever hope to achieve. I had spent the past five hours laboring with heaving breaths up and down a yak trail deep in the Himalayas. This was the third week of a journey that had taken me to a half-dozen villages where I was organizing educational programs for neglected children.

Prior to the appearance of the old man, I had been trying to catch my breath while staring, spellbound, at five of the highest mountain peaks in the world.

I was debating whether I had the energy to pull out my camera for another quick shot when the Sherpa who was acting as a guide rushed up to me.

"Sir," he said to me, "you help man." This was not a question but rather a direct order. It was all the more remarkable because the guide was usually so deferential, if not obsequious.

I approached the old man cautiously, not exactly sure what was expected of me, nor how I was supposed to help him. Once I got closer, I could see more closely his swollen hand that was so covered with blisters it looked like a balloon about to burst. There were white, pus-filled sores running along his fingers and palm, almost as if there were caterpillars crawling underneath his skin.

The old man was a dignified gentleman, dressed in a white shirt, vest, and tights, a long knife at his side. He was an impressive figure, all the more so because although his hand was grossly disfigured, he was obviously under great control of the crippling pain.

"You help him," the Sherpa said again, pointing to the old man's hand.

The old man looked at me and managed a smile between his tight lips. He held out his hand as if it was a foreign object that belonged to someone else. He turned it one way, then the other, displaying the network of bloated blisters that covered both sides.

"What happened?" I asked, partially out of curiosity, but also to stall for time before I could figure out what I was supposed to do. I was no doctor, at least not a real one. The last thing in the world this guy needed right now was a psychologist.

The old man and the Sherpa spoke for several minutes before it was announced with simple clarity: "Boiling water."

"He spilled boiling water on himself?" I asked. "Is that what happened?"

Both men nodded.

Because I was a foreigner, it was common for locals to believe that I possessed medical supplies and expertise that far exceeded their own meager resources. They were not far wrong, considering that the nearest medical facility was a two-day walk away. If this man did not receive help from me, he would most likely have to deal with this on his own.

I looked into my supplies and found a supply of gauze and antiseptic cream which I proceeded to apply to the blistered hand. No matter how delicately I spread the lotion I could hear the man's involuntary gasps. Adopting the manner of the doctor that I was now pretending to be, I handed him aspirin to take for the pain. "Take two of these now, another two before you go to bed tonight." I felt myself stifling a nervous giggle once I realized I was reciting the line from some doctor show on television.

The old man looked at me with genuine gratitude, as if I had just saved his life, or at least his hand. He brought his hands up to his chin, forming the steeple gesture of respect in this part of the world. "*Namaste*," he said, then turned and headed back up the slope with his hand still held aloft.

I walked on for the rest of the day, up and down more mountains, through rice paddies and mustard fields, passing herds of water buffalo, troops of monkeys, mule trains, and porters on this Himalayan highway. All the major Annapurna peaks were visible throughout the day, draped in clouds. There was more scenery and stimulation than anyone could ever hope to encounter in a lifetime. Yet I couldn't get that old man and his hand out of my mind. I was haunted by that encounter, and I couldn't figure out why it had such a huge impact on me.

Then it came to me: I fixed something. At least, I think I did. Surely I hadn't done any harm in my brief foray as an emergency physician. Even if the aspirin and antiseptic didn't make much of a difference, I know—I am *certain*—that my words of reassurance soothed the man's pain.

I am someone who has no mechanical aptitude whatsoever. I can barely change the batteries in my camera and flashlight. I often break light bulbs while changing them. I am more than unusually proud that I can change a flat tire; in some ways, I look forward to those episodes, because in an hour I can fix something, make it better.

So it is that I chose a profession in which I am rarely sure that I ever really help anyone. Even when I do think I make a difference, I'm never quite certain whether the effects will really last, or even if my clients are just reporting imaginary progress. Most of the work I do, as a teacher or supervisor or clinician, takes many weeks, months, or even years, before I see substantial, visible changes.

Yet in about 15 minutes, I dressed the wound of someone in need and helped him to feel better. I have no idea, of course, what happened to the man after our paths diverged. Maybe he lost the use of his hand or even died of infection. But I'd like to think that, regardless of my rather simplistic attempt at practicing medicine without a license, I eased his suffering in ways that I long for every day with my clients and students. I know it isn't my job to make people feel better but, rather, to help them to take better care of themselves and take greater charge of their own lives—even though this often means stirring up *more* pain. I suppose that also fits what happened when I caused more pain in the old man by cleaning and treating his wounds in order to prevent infection and aid healing.

There are times when I feel such despair at what it is that I try to do. Some of the people we all attempt to help have problems that are so long-standing, so chronic and unremitting, so severe, that whatever we do seems like nothing but a token gesture. The kids leave the session and return to their gangs or abusive homes. Those with impulse disorders, hallucinations, personality disturbances, chronic drug abuse, major depression—the list goes on and on—sometimes seem impervious to the most powerful interventions. When some of our most challenging cases do show definite signs of progress, we are left to wonder how much of these changes will persist over time, especially with a return to dysfunctional environments, abject poverty, or crime-filled neighborhoods.

Just once in awhile it feels so glorious to fix someone or something—to *know* that I really helped someone. That this experience of fixing a hand took place during such a brief interval is even more of a gift. It is also a clear indication of my own need to feel useful, how my own sense of potency, as a person and a professional, comes from continually proving that I have not lost my power. With each new person I help, I wonder whether the magic has left me, whether I have anything left to give.

I am forced to confront the sense of powerlessness I have felt most of my life, the drive that has led me—pushed me—to be so overachieving, to prove myself again and again. I realize now that my interaction with the old man wasn't really about fixing his hand. He was the latest opportunity that I used to try and fix myself.

As I now relive this incident, I'm not certain the Sherpa begged me to help this old man as much as I jumped at the chance to do something useful for him. I needed this encounter. It had been more than a week on the trail in which people were taking care of me, rather than the configuration that I am used to—being responsible for taking care of others. Without such constant opportunities to be helpful, I feel like I am losing my way, even losing myself.

I tried to fix the old man's hand and felt a degree of satisfaction to an extent that I rarely experience in teaching or counseling. Partly, this resulted from the immediate feedback that my intervention was effective. But it was also because my "client" would have had no other recourse if I had not been on the scene. It was as if I arrived at that exact time and place, in one of the most remote places in the world, specifically to do something useful.

I hardly have to travel halfway around the world to make a difference. It just feels like the magnitude and intensity of the experience was amplified by the novelty of what, with whom, and how it took place. It gets me thinking that I try to find my way by taking new, undiscovered paths that allow me to access new parts of myself. I only bandaged a wound, yet in so doing, I also healed myself.

In this book, you will read many other stories similar to mine, undertaken by fairly ordinary people (many of them students) who felt inspired to exercise their altruistic spirit and get involved in promoting social justice projects on a local or global scale. You will hear this theme repeated many times in your educational career, since it is currently a very hot trend to encourage, if not require, students to become involved in some type of service learning. It is reasoned that there is only so much you can learn in a classroom or in books — the wide world awaits you, with many challenges and opportunities.

WHAT IS SOCIAL JUSTICE ANYWAY?

No, it isn't a gathering of judges getting together for drinks and conversation, nor is it a particularly gregarious and fun-loving judge. It also does not refer to legal proceedings at a social function. With that said about what it is *not*, social justice is a bit difficult to clearly define. It is one of those terms that is thrown around all the time, variously referring to righting wrongs, taking a moral stand, or fighting against some perceived injustice. Some fringe groups also use the term to refer to any cause that promotes their radical vision of what is fair and right (Lum, 2007).

Within the context of the social or hard sciences, health, business, or any other profession, "social justice" is used often to describe altruistic efforts in some capacity, such as advocating on behalf of those without a voice or for greater equity. For instance, the tragedy that occurred on 9/11 with the terrorist attacks on the World Trade Center and the Pentagon mobilized tremendous compassion for the families of the 5,000 people who died, yet 10 times that number of children die of starvation and malnutrition *every day*. During the hour or so that you spent reading this book, another 400 children died, most of whom could have been saved if they had access to health care and a nutritious food supply.

Eyes Closed Shut

I love warm water, hot sand, and beautiful women. I can't help it, it's my weakness. During spring break one year I came down here to Cancun with some friends, and never left. I got a job full time as a cabana boy for Club Med, and it's the best. I basically get paid to just be on vacation. I've been doing it for five years now, and for most of the time I've just stayed on the grounds of the resort. Last year I met a girl here who works in the restaurant. She's actually from the Yucatan, and grew up down the coast from here, just north of Belize. She's beautiful, not like anyone I've ever met, but she comes from this really poor background. I've been down to visit her family a few times, and it has just blown my mind to see how much poverty they're living in. They have food to eat and all that, but it's not exactly the cleanest, most sanitary living conditions. Everything stinks like sewage, and there are flies everywhere. The roof on their home isn't very good, and when it rains everyone gets wet. It's so weird driving from Club Med in Cancun down the Yucatan to visit them. I just can't believe the gap between the people at the resort and these people, and it's only a two-hour drive away. If the people at Club Med could even just put a little resources and effort and help, that entire village could be fixed up, but I don't even know if anyone knows of its existence. I think that is the way most of us live our lives—with our eyes closed to what's going on around us.

As multifaceted and broadly applied as the term might be, social justice generally can be described as having any of the following characteristics or actions (Fouad, Gerstein, & Toporek, 2006; Lee & Hipolito-Delgado, 2007):

1. *Challenging* systemic inequities within an organization or community. This involves first *recognizing* that some individuals or groups are marginalized in some way and then *doing something* to change the status quo.
2. *Transforming* social institutions. Once inequities are identified, steps are taken to change the ways that schools, agencies, government departments, and other organizations operate.
3. *Inviting* fuller access to resources and full participation on the part of excluded people. Again, this involves constructive *action* (rather than mere talk) to advocate on behalf of those without equal rights because of their

race, age, religion, gender, disability, sexual orientation, education, socio-economic status, or group membership.

4. *Bringing attention* to issues of oppression, prejudice, and social inequities within an organization or community.

5. *Combating* racism, prejudice, homophobia, ageism, and sexism as it is witnessed. Speaking out and taking action in the face of injustices and oppression.

6. *Advocating* on behalf of human rights, especially among those who have minority status or who have been historically denied privileges afforded to

Becoming involved in some type of social justice or service learning experience can be structured according to your own interests, passions, experience, goals, time availability, and resources. But it does take considerable initiative, personal sacrifice, and a degree of personal challenge to work in communities without the familiarity and comforts to which you have become accustomed.

those of the majority. For example, this could refer to Native Americans, African Americans, and other minorities within the United States, those of the "untouchable" caste in India, the Kurds of Iraq, the hill tribes of Cambodia, the Palestinians in the Middle East, and so on.

7. *Empowering* those who have historically been without a voice. This may involve personal self-sacrifice, as well as surrendering some of your own privileges and advantages.

8. *Volunteering time and devoting personal resources* to make a difference among those most in need. Whether this is with the homeless in your own community or with those most at-risk across the nation or abroad, you develop and implement strategies for making a difference.

Making Difficult Choices

I grew up in the Bronx. The boys in school never liked me, calling me "The Smart Girl," and that gave me an edge. I didn't like anyone, and no one really liked me, so I just kept to myself. I put all that aggression into studying, and at my school there wasn't a lot of competition, so I was first in my class. My school counselor said that with my grades I could get into Harvard, because they were looking for "disadvantaged students" or something like that. Anyway, I applied, got in, and now it's my fourth year here. I chose to study urban planning because there is a lot of math in that, and math has always been easy for me. When I graduate, I can pretty much get any job I want. Hell, I can even go to Beverly Hills in California and do urban planning for all the rich people. My family thinks I should come back to the Bronx and help our area to make it more suitable for living. Part of me wants to go home to help, but part of me thinks, "screw them!" The people in my neighborhood weren't exactly helpful to me growing up, so why should I go back and help them now? My mother says "to whom much is given, much is expected," or some crap like that. I know I have an amazing life in front of me, but I think if I moved to California my mother's voice would always be ringing in the back of my head. I think I have to stay, and try to make a difference where I grew up.

When you combine all of these dimensions, what emerges is a vision of social justice in which professionals in a variety of fields act as advocates, activists, and leaders in the cause of promoting human freedom and equality. Regardless of where you end up working, and what you end up doing for a living, there will be countless opportunities for you to stand up for the rights of those who are oppressed. For those of you who are more ambitious in this enterprise, there are also limitless possibilities for you to visit places where oppression, poverty, and injustice are the norm. This book tells the story of some such efforts on the part of individuals who are not that different from you.

CHAPTER 2

The Dance of Hope

The children had formed a gauntlet, beginning where we were standing by the truck that brought us to this village and stretching in two parallel, undulating lines to the entrance of the one-room school. The children were calling out in a chanting rhythm, beckoning us to walk through the line.

We approached the squirming tunnel of children, feeling both embarrassed and flattered to be the center of attention. As we walked between the two lines, the children showered us with flowers. The older, taller kids placed garlands of flowers around our necks; smaller children placed bouquets in our hands. The tiniest kids, some just out of toddlerhood, tossed handfuls of petals as far as their little arms could throw. As we made our way through the line, we were covered in the fragrant petals.

Finally, we reached the schoolhouse, a single room constructed of concrete blocks. Inside, it was dark, the only light coming from a single bulb hanging from the ceiling. There were wooden pews in a row, perhaps ten in all, and they were packed with people. There were village elders in attendance, the chief, the school principal and teacher, parents, and half a dozen students with their families. One old woman, who was barely ambulatory, managed to crawl along the floor where the crowd made space for her.

We were in the village of Saranpur, an isolated community of several thousand in the southern region of Nepal. The Maoist rebels were active in this area, so we had been forced to travel by small plane from Kathmandu and then by rutted, back roads occupied by tractors, goats, water buffalo, and bicycles.

Children in the village of Saranpur, located in the remote Chitwan region of Nepal, line up to welcome guests who have arrived to distribute scholarships to lower-caste children who would otherwise not be able to attend school.

Machine gun nests were perched on the top of bridges, intending to stop the rebel advance. Yet when we crossed to the other side of the bridge, the Maoists were waiting with their own gun emplacements, also extorting a "fee" to cross their territory. There were army roadblocks set up everywhere, as well as curfews, but in this part of the country the people were only concerned with survival; the politics of the Maoists escaped them (it was only later that we would come face to face with the rebels in the Himalayas, where they extorted money to guarantee safe passage).

Originally, we had traveled to Nepal to help introduce counseling methods to the medical community and to supervise a research project exploring why so many mothers die giving birth. In Nepal, the vast majority of people do not have access to any medical care whatsoever. They have among the highest maternal and infant mortality rates in the world. There are villages where goiters from nutrition deficiencies are so common that the residents have come to see the huge balls growing out of their necks as attractive. In fact, anyone without a prominent goiter is viewed as a freak.

Several of us in the group had already delivered lectures to health ministers, government officials, health administrators, physicians, and nurses about the value of counseling methods. In the whole country, there are a few dozen psychiatrists and psychologists and counselors for a population of more than 30 million. That means that each mental health professional has a caseload of over a million each!

We had met with hospital staff and health care workers to discuss ways they could integrate the interventions that seemed best suited to the Nepalese context. While this work was satisfying, even warmly received, the real reason we had come so far was to visit this village.

Working with Nepalese friends and colleagues, we were establishing a new scholarship program for the neglected children of Nepal. The girls, especially, were afforded very few opportunities for education. Many were kidnapped by sex slavers or sold by their families for indentured work, often ending up in the brothels of northern India.

One of us (Jeffrey) had been doing research with a Nepalese obstetrician, Kiran Regmi, on ways to encourage more women to seek medical care. Many women were dying because they were unwilling to visit health care facilities. They did not want male doctors to touch their bodies. They did not feel respected in these places. They felt like objects that were merely shuffled around.

One way we might change these attitudes was, first, to teach physicians to be more interpersonally responsive. Second, our job was to help promote more opportunities for girls to become doctors themselves and perhaps break the tragic cycle. If we could launch a foundation, contributing some of our own money as start-up capital, we could help keep more children in school. We had already contributed enough money that we were about to award the first six scholarships. And that is why the schoolhouse was packed on this day: the village was celebrating the birth of hope.

As we sat at the honored place in the room, covered in our garlands of flowers, we could not help but think about the work we do as counselors and teachers back home. Helping others is what we teach in the classroom, yet often the interaction is one-to-one. Sitting in this school, it seemed clear that this was a community intervention and interaction.

"You have gathered here today to honor us," Jeffrey addressed the village assembly. "But we are here to honor *you*. There are times when you must feel that nobody cares about you." Jeffrey spoke slowly, waiting for the translation. "I wish you to know that the people of America do care about you, and about your children. They want to help you keep your children in school, because that is the only way they can have a future."

Speaking directly to the children next, Jeffrey told them that we would do what we could to help them, but they must work hard to study and learn. It was a solid message, but I had no way of knowing how it was heard and understood. One thing that we did see clearly was the look of pride on the children's faces when each came up to accept the scholarship that would allow him or her to remain in school for another year.

After the ceremony ended, everyone piled out of the cramped schoolhouse. Thinking we were now off the hook, we melted into the crowd. Yet the festivities were only beginning. The women of the community began to form a circle, chanting at first, then singing. Drummers pounded a beat and the women began to dance, swaying their bodies and moving their hands hypnotically.

One member of our group was pulled into the circle and pressed to join the dance. Holding his hands out to his side, he imitated the women's movements as best he could. Yet the most extraordinary sight of all was watching Dr. Kiran, the senior gynecologist, dancing with the girls and women. Seeing a doctor dance with her patients was a powerfully compelling image, one that ensured that this was one place where the women would seek their doctor's help during times of need. As Kiran danced, the girls and women smiled, laughed, kept motioning the dance to continue. It appeared that each glance towards Kiran was a look of acknowledgement that here was one doctor who understood the true lives of her patients and was not so far above them that she could not actually be part of the community. They would come to her, despite her being a doctor, because of her empathy and her willingness to be with people in their real lives.

We climbed into the truck for the long journey back to the central district of Chitwan. We looked out the back window to see the children, and their parents, watching the strangers depart. What were they thinking now, we wondered? What did they make of all this?

As a physician in a rural area without regular health care, Kiran must earn the trust of the village women if she is to have any impact. She must deal with competition from the local shaman, who can sometimes be helpful but just as often can be dangerous.

We sat quietly during the return, keeping our thoughts to ourselves. After some time dodging various livestock, rickshaws, and pedestrians, we came upon a solitary Buddhist monk walking along the road. Dressed in a burgundy robe, held together by a rope around the middle, he glanced at us as we slowed to a stop by his side. The monk's face lit up in a smile as he made eye contact with each one of us. Then he reached inside and handed us a glutinous ball. Each of us broke off a small piece to taste the sweet offering. Then, without another glance, the monk continued his journey.

Even now, we can still taste the gritty sweetness in our mouths, just as we can smell the flowers that had been placed around our necks. We are still haunted by the final view of the villagers watching us drive away, wondering if we would forget them, if we would ever return, if we would keep our promises to help them.

Joining the Dance

It isn't necessary to travel to the remote Himalayan Republic of Nepal to participate in a dance of hope. Within your own community, there are many people who feel neglected and forgotten. What continues to linger most from this first journey is the possibility of what one person can do to make a difference. But first, you must join the dance.

Watching People Suffer

When I was four years old, my parents dropped me off at an orphanage and then hit the hippie trail to California. I guess it was a typical 1970s story, but my sister and I are the other side of the equation. We're the kids who got left behind, that you didn't see at Woodstock. We were shipped from one home to another for most of our childhood, with no sense of grounding or anything. Try being the new kid in school every six months. You get used to defending yourself pretty quick. But the other day I read about the child soldiers in Uganda. These kids can't even stay in their homes, or else rebel leaders will kidnap them to put in their armies. They walk miles every single night, and sleep under bridges, just so they don't get kidnapped. This just blew my mind! I mean, I know a little of this stuff, but compared to them I'm like a kid from the 'burbs. I had to worry about getting beat up in school, but they actually have to be worried about getting killed—every single night! Sometimes when I think about it, my stomach wants to explode, and I know I have to do something to help. I feel like they're my brothers over there, and I'm just watching them suffer.

Each of us has admired the work of large charitable and social justice organizations that have helped change the shape of our world. Yet we've remained frustrated with the bureaucracies and skeptical toward the wasteful spending, high overhead, and huge size of these projects. In many developing countries, you can immediately spot the "do-gooders" because they are staying in the most expensive hotels and driving around in Land Rovers. Within many of the most well-known charities and social service agencies (we won't mention names), expenses can exceed 75 percent or the funds that are raised. Once political corruption and bribes are added to the picture, very little of the resources actually reach the people for which they were intended.

The other thing that is most daunting for beginners who wish to become involved in activism, social justice, charity, or altruistic work is how easily you can become lost within the huge organization that may employ tens of thousands. It is hard to measure your impact and difficult to determine what kind of effect you, personally, may be having. This is what led each of us to start our own modest efforts, and we hope it will encourage you to do the same in some stage or aspect of your life.

BENEFITS OF VOLUNTEERING

The idea of serving those who are less fortunate than ourselves is not restricted to helping professionals. The fastest growing segment of the travel market is called *voluntourism*, in which people devote part or all of their vacations to some kind of altruistic activity (Wearing, 2001). There are hundreds of organizations that provide opportunities for vacationers to work in a variety of projects, depending on their interests and expertise in such fields as construction, medicine, education, community development, archaeology, and child welfare.

Time to Hit the Road

All right, I've got three months until college graduation and I am psyched out of my mind. I've been living in books for what seems like my whole life and now I'll be done with studying forever! I truly hated school—if I see another book I'm going to freak out. I'm just ready to get out into the world, have fun, and explore. I'm ready, but I don't really know what the hell I'm going to do. I majored in communications, so I guess that taught me how to communicate or something, but it's not like I can really use it for anything. I was trying to get that piece of paper, man. You know? When my dad was this age he took off to live in India for a year. He also had no idea what to do with his life, but for some reason thought India would be a good place to start. It was the 1970s and all that hippie stuff, so I guess that was the normal thing to do. My dad's pretty much my hero. He's had a great life, and he thinks I should go travel somewhere because he thinks it will help me grow up. So that's what I'm going to do. I'm not sure where I'm going yet, but I know that I just need to get out there and see things for myself.

Research has distinguished between two types of individuals who devote their time to service: those who are "volunteer-minded" versus those who are "vacation-minded." Whereas the former seeks an extended mission or service as a main priority, the latter intends to spend a portion of vacation time doing something useful (Brown & Morrison, 2003). Interestingly, even those who are merely dabbling in a few days of service work as a diversion from their holiday plans still report universally that this is the best part of their trip (Brown & Lehto, 2005).

A number of studies have found that volunteering to help in a foreign land provide a number of benefits for those who participate in projects (Broad, 2003; Stebbins & Graham, 2004; Thoits & Hewitt, 2001).

- Sense of purpose
- Contemplation
- Broadened interests
- Social interaction
- Belonging
- Flexibility

People who volunteer their time to meaningful causes are more healthy than those who do not. They experience less depression, exhibit higher self-esteem and self-control, report greater personal fulfillment, and feel more relaxed and satisfied with their lives (Brown & Lehto, 2005). In a review of studies examining the health benefits of altruistic volunteers who work on behalf of charitable causes, Oman (2007) found the most consistent result was greater longevity—people who devote their time to helping others live longer. They are also better functioning in physical health, more active, and less prone to illness (Post, 2007). This is even after people studied are adjusted for differences in income, demographics, employment and other such factors. Apart from actual health benefits, volunteers report greater well-being, higher emotional functioning, and less social isolation (Schwartz, 2007).

GIVE AS WELL AS TAKE

One of the major themes of this book is that by giving to others, you also profit yourself. Most travel memories are not enduring because they were "only"

Realizing What I Want to Do

I just switched my major to social work, and my parents are absolutely freaking out. My old major was finance, which I guess is a really stable, traditional major. My parents aren't rich, and they're having a hard time paying for my tuition, so I guess I understand why they would want me to study something that could make me a lot of money. But I hate it! I just can't stand it and it drives me mad. I'm not a numbers person, and last year I read that book about a guy who builds schools for kids in Afghanistan. His story was amazing! He has such an exciting life, and he is actually making a difference. That's what I want to do, and I don't care if I don't make any money doing it.

vacations, only time-outs from daily routines. When you make an effort to extend yourself to others in altruistic ways, there is considerable evidence that you experience a kind of "helper's high" that results in feelings of exhilaration and goodwill (Kottler, 2000).

Altruistic behavior is one of the features of our species in which we are sometimes inclined to give of ourselves to others, even against our own best interests (Scott & Seglow, 2008). Even animals have been known to sacrifice themselves for the benefit of the flock or herd, signaling to their brethren against a predator. For example, individual monkeys will distract a lion, "volunteering" as prey, so that the rest of the troop can escape (Gould & Marler, 1987). A squirrel will signal the sighting of a hawk, making itself the designated target so that others can find safe shelter (Sherman, 1980). Certain species of bees and spiders will launch suicide missions to protect the hive or nest from invaders (Barber, 2004).

Yet humans often make conscious rather than instinctual choices to give of their time, money, resources, energy, or even their lives to benefit those who are less fortunate. And we are even willing to do this for perfect strangers with whom we share no kinship bonds nor can ever expect reciprocal favors. Good Samaritans rescue strangers from burning buildings, overturned vehicles, or crashed planes, sometimes dying in their heroic gestures. Millionaires give away their money. Priests, nuns, and monks devote their whole lives to serving others. And college students, who could otherwise invest their time and efforts into learning how to make a fortune in business, decide on professions that allow them to help others.

One of the themes we have explored in this book is that it is not necessary to be heroic, or take on a major enterprise, or to initiate some sort of large-scale project to make an important difference in our lives, much less in the lives of others. There is a saying from the Talmud, one of the ancient Hebrew books, that if you save just one life, it is as if you have saved the whole world. In this sacred text, the spirit of service, of giving to others, is considered the highest calling. This same message is found within almost all the world's religions.

I Couldn't Just Stand There

Last year I was walking home from school and came across some old man beating on his dog. It wasn't a normal punishment; he was really hurting the little guy. I'm not exactly a dog lover, but I just couldn't believe what I was seeing. It was a really weird moment when I knew I could just keep walking, or I could try to do something. I ended up calling the police and stayed there until they arrived to make sure the guy got busted. It was crazy! I ended up having to go to court for months just to make sure this guy got punished since I was the only real witness. Ever since then I've been excited about social service and trying to help others. If that one man was beating on his dog, imagine all the people out there who are doing even worse things. I never thought about this before because I just wasn't exposed to it, but now that I've been I feel like I just have to be helping in some way.

Traveling is often an enterprise characterized primarily by the process of "taking in." The whole point of going on tours, visiting museums, taking photos, buying souvenirs, contracting for adventures, covering territory, climbing mountains, swimming with dolphins, is to accumulate new experiences; in a sense, you are attempting to enrich your own life through the consumption of experience. Yet when there is both give and take, travel can become even more meaningful on multiple levels.

Among the most commonly identified motives for engaging in *voluntourism*, especially among the student population, are some themes that may be familiar to you:

1. *Personal ambition*. There is nothing wrong with having a self-serving motive in helping activities, that is, to build a resume or gain professional experience that will make you more marketable in the future. In fact, people with such personal goals often devote more time and commitment to their volunteer work than do others who are driven purely by altruism alone (Winerman, 2006). When you have a clear personal agenda that you wish to attain, especially goals that can be realistically met within the planned volunteer experience, you are more likely to feel satisfied afterwards. Those who are disappointed by their volunteer efforts tend to be people who had unreasonable objectives that could never be met—like wiping out poverty or saving a village (Clary et al., 1998).

2. *Enhancement of self-esteem*. There is an element to volunteering for many people that involves a search for self. During times when you may feel lost, uncertain, or without direction, traveling to a new place to do something useful may open new doors of self-awareness and understanding. Improved confidence and resourcefulness are often reported after such experiences. Those who left home in the first place to escape pressure, stress, or unfinished business may return with a different perspective that allows them to address the issues in more fully functioning ways.

3. *Personal growth*. This can take place within a multitude of areas, including the intellectual, moral, social, emotional, and interpersonal domains. You are likely to make new friends, become exposed to new environments, and stretch yourself in ways that did not seem possible. You develop a degree of flexibility and resilience that hopefully, upon your return, you can apply to new challenges that you face.

4. *Justice and empathy*. Quite simply, it feels good to help others who are in need. It feels good to be useful, to do something that you know makes a difference in the world. Such efforts give life greater meaning.

Making a Difference

I've had a problem with depression since I was a little kid. Everyone was out there on the playground, and I just wanted to sit in the corner by myself. Everything just seemed dark to me. I didn't even know why people liked trying to have fun; it just all seemed so stupid. All through most of college I felt this way, too—everything just seemed so fake and ridiculous. My grades weren't that good, either, so once I was out of college I didn't have that many options. I thought I would try teaching, because the hours are good and you have summers off, but no decent high school would hire me. The only place I could get a job was in the ghetto, which I really didn't want to do, but I had no other option really. As it turns out, I *love* this job. It may be the first thing in my life that I actually have ever loved. The kids don't come from rosy backgrounds, so they aren't trying to out-fake each other with the latest car or something like that. They are totally real and deal with crap that I could never have imagined. And I feel like I'm making a difference in their lives. I never thought this would change me as much as it has.

Each of us is not only a member of a family, a tribe, a race, a religion, or a club; we are all citizens of the world. Each of us is responsible for the plight of every other person, no matter where they reside. In one sense, there is a moral obligation that many people feel to do good for others, without regard to personal benefits. It is a way to reach beyond our own self-interest, our own egocentric worlds, and to do something significant to make the world a better place for all, especially those who had the misfortune to be born into poverty, war, or abuse.

I COULDN'T MAKE THIS UP

I (Jeffrey) work in a place that looks like the way the rest of the world will look in 20 years. It looks like the United Nations, a gathering of people from all around the world speaking hundreds of different languages. Like most of Southern California, we are a community of immigrants. In our program at the university, about one-third of the students are from Central and South America, one-third from Asia, and one-third "other," meaning they are

African as well as African American, Middle Eastern, Eastern European, and Caucasian.

When I walk around campus I see many interracial couples holding hands, sitting under palm trees studying, or on their way to classes. Most are first-generation college students. Most speak a language other than English at home. And more and more, the boundaries between their cultural differences are collapsing.

One of my jobs as a department chair is to stand on stage during the graduation ceremony and read the names of students as they retrieve their diplomas. Weeks before the date, I print out a list of all the students who will be graduating. I research, from multiple sources, the correct pronunciations, as I know that there is nothing more embarrassing then having one's name mangled, on such an important day, and in front of all one's families and friends. In most cases, this is the first family member to ever receive a master's degree, much less to ever have attended college.

Once I have the list in hand, I practice saying the names aloud for hours and hours (I'm not making this up). I have other faculty members listen and critique my performance. I practice not only the correct enunciation of each name, but also the flow of words. And I do this not only because I am a perfectionist and a little compulsive (which I am) but because the job is so challenging. Why, you might ask, is reading the list of graduates such a difficult task? The answer is cross-cultural romance, or to say that differently, intermarriage.

So many of our students are living with partners who are of a different race, ethnicity, and religion than their own. The cumulative effect of such increasingly cultural-blind relationships is that my list contains names like Rosarita Nguyen, Michal Hernandez, Samanaz McClendaghan, May Ho Chen-Chhetri. The hyphenated names are especially killer tongue-twisters for me.

I sit on the stage after my job is done, feeling proud of our students who have completed their studies while overcoming so many hardships; I also feel proud of myself for having gotten through the list with reasonable fluency (although I still mangled a few). I see all the different races and ethnicities of the families sitting in the audience, so many of whom are immigrants one generation removed.

Speaking of immigrants, we had a discussion in my culture class last night about the hardships of adjusting to a new culture. One of the advantages of working in such a culturally diverse place is that I rarely have to reach into a textbook for examples of any concept we might want to examine. We were talking about the challenges that counselors face trying to work with clients who come to them from such different backgrounds. For clients, as well, they often feel as if they are in a foreign land. We speak a different language in counseling. We have unique customs and rituals. We expect certain behaviors that would not be appropriate in other contexts.

I asked members of the class if they could draw on their own experience as immigrants to tell a story of the challenges they faced adjusting to a new country.

A Nepalese student immediately spoke up. She mentioned how stunned she was after her arrival to discover that people in this country don't remove their shoes before entering a dwelling.

"That's very interesting," another student chimed in, an Israeli. "I remember when I first came here I went to someone's house for a visit and she asked me to take off my shoes before I came into her house. I thought this was very peculiar as we would never do this in Israel. But then I figured that this was the custom here."

Everyone in the class started laughing.

"No," she said. "That's not all. So then some time later I visited another friend who watched me take off my shoes. She told me later that she thought that was an Israeli custom to remove one's shoes."

I'm not making this up. This happened last night.

So, I'm sitting in my office today musing about these interesting cultural understandings between couples in their relationships and misunderstandings between people of different groups who are trying hard to fit in. What does all this mean? I wondered. I'm supposed to be an expert on this stuff and I can barely pronounce the names of my students. How am I supposed to find my way as a practitioner, much less as a supervisor and teacher, when cultural differences are so profound?

Before I could come to any sort of conclusion, a student walked in my office and asked if she could speak with me.

"Sure," I answered, and invited her to sit down.

She then proceeded to tell me that she was extremely unhappy, if not depressed. "My marriage is not a good one," she pronounced. "I respect my husband, but I do not love him. He is a good man but we have nothing in common. He does not talk to me about things. He does not seem to care about the things that I care about."

I was just about to ask her what, then, was she doing with him, when I stopped and remembered what I was thinking about just as she entered the office. There is a cultural context for this story and I was about to overlook it, just as I tell my students never to do.

"I see," I said neutrally. "And what is that like for you?" Nice, ambiguous question. Gives me time to stall. No implied value judgment.

She then went on to tell me that her marriage had been arranged by her parents, that love was not always a component of marriage in her country, and that respect was far more important.

"You said your marriage is not a good one," I reflected back, sort of confronting her, but also not wanting to get very deeply into these issues with someone who was not a client.

"That is so, but I would like to know how to make it better."

Whew. Close call. I referred her to a counselor and reassured her that this was a good thing to do. But I thought how close I might have been to spouting the party line of "American" values: "Oh, you're not happy in your marriage? You don't love your husband? Well then, why not think about an alternative?"

Hey, I thought, maybe I'm not as ignorant as I often feel about this cultural stuff. I travel a lot, work in other countries. Heck, I *teach* culture to students.

Feeling self-satisfied about the conversation I next turned to my computer to catch up on e-mail. The third message I read was from a doctoral student I'm working with in Nepal, who also happens to be a gynecologist working in rural areas. This was her message:

A week ago a woman came to see me in the hospital in great pain. Her whole uterus, together with a full-term baby, had prolapsed through her vagina. Somehow I managed to deliver the baby through a cesarean section. But the uterus was still outside the vagina and would have to remain there for another seven to eight days until further surgery was possible. She would need to remain in the hospital for at least another two weeks.

The woman insisted that she had to go home. When I asked her what was so important that she was going to risk her health, if not her life, she told me that she had to attend the delivery of her goat.

So my question, Jeffrey, is how would you counsel such a person?

I stared at the computer for far too long, trying to frame some sort of response. I couldn't believe all the critical incidents that I had experienced in the previous 24 hours. My head hurt. What do you say to someone whose cultural values place the birth of her goat's kid over that of her own health?

So I didn't answer her because I didn't know what to say. Instead I went to Nepal to see what I could do to help. And I'm not making this up.

CHAPTER 3

Children Disappearing

In this chapter, we tell the first of several stories of social justice projects in action. These were hardly strategically planned activities that were meticulously organized. Rather, they were the result of serendipitous events in which we came face-to-face with a need that we were each in a position to address in a limited, casual way. From that first gesture offering help, the projects grew into full-fledged organizations with dozens of staff and a global mission. But we are getting way ahead of ourselves. It all begins with the awareness of a problem, one that *you* may be in a position to do something about.

A NATION ON THE VERGE OF COLLAPSE

Nepal is a country known primarily as the host for mountaineers who aspire to climb the highest peaks in the world. Thousands of climbers travel to the Himalayas each spring for the privilege of paying six figures just to climb Everest and then say they did—or tried, anyway. One guy, a rich Texan, forked over $400,000 for his extravagant budget so he could enjoy elaborate meals catered at 20,000 feet. When questioned about how he could throw away a small fortune in such self-indulgence, surrounded by millions of starving people, he commented: "But what else was I gonna do—buy myself another boat?" (Fedarko, 2007, p. 110).

Nepal is among the poorest nations in the world and is ranked amongst the 10 least-developed countries by the United Nations. The average person earns about $1 per day. Life expectancy is 57 years, compared to 75 for developed countries. Most of the citizens eat two meals a day consisting of *dal bat*, a scoop

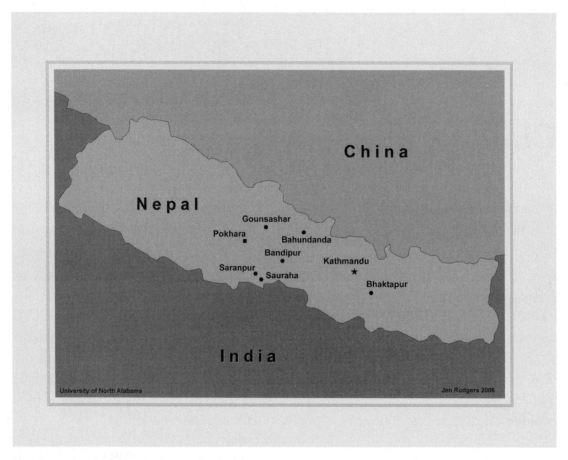

Nepal is a landlocked country sandwiched between the two Asian superpowers. It is bordered on the north by the Himalayan mountain range and on the south by lowland jungles. There are dozens of different ethnic groups and hundreds of languages spoken. You may have heard of a few of these tribes: the *Sherpas*, who are famous as mountain climbers, and the *Gurkhas*, who are known as fierce warriors who have fought along the British in many of the world's conflicts.

The capital city of Kathmandu and the main tourist center of Pokhara are shown on the map, along with several of the villages that are discussed in this book. Most of Nepal practices the Hindu religion, similar to their Indian neighbors to the south, although Buddhism is the dominant region in the north near what used to be Tibet (and is now part of China).

of rice with a spoon of watery lentils on top. In rural areas, many people don't have shoes, even in the high Himalayas. Even for tourists and trekkers, the most enduring image of a visit to this country may not be the pristine mountain scenery but shoeless porters carrying 150-pound loads on their backs, children in villages with huge goiters growing out of their necks, and mothers begging, not for money, but for aspirin. In the remote villages of Nepal, if someone has a serious infection, a burst appendix, or a serious medical problem, and there is not enough time to walk three days to the nearest day-long bus trip into the capital city, they die.

Nepal has one of the highest infant and child mortality rates in the world. Additionally, many women die during childbirth; maternal mortality is 550 deaths per 100,000 live births, compared to 7 or 8 in most developed countries. Nepal ranks among the worst in the world in basic health care services; 90% of the population does not have access to adequate medical care. In addition to widespread malnutrition and infectious diseases, HIV is becoming an increasing problem. Sex slavers kidnap or buy young girls in rural areas and transport them back to brothels in India, where Indian men believe that having sex with virgins will cure them of AIDS and other sexually transmitted infections. After several years of captivity, the girls are then sent back to their villages, where they pass the infection on to others.

On top of its other problems, Nepal happens to be located strategically between China and India. Maoist insurgents had been trying for more than a decade to start a revolution until the monarchy was abolished in 2008. Tibetan nationalists have been using it as a staging ground for their own plans to wrest their country back from the Chinese. The King, Queen, and royal family were murdered by the Crown Prince. The economic and political situation is highly unstable.

With the regional instability and a downturn in global tourism, in particular from the United States due to threats of international terrorism, the tourism industry has been crippled, leading to economic disaster. It is estimated that in many villages, close to 40 families live off the annual income of one *Sherpa* (mountain guide). The reduction in income from tourism is affecting the health and well-being of many families, with malnutrition increasing among both children and adults. As a result, ordinary infections that are easily curable become life threatening.

Clearly, this is a nation with tremendous political, economic, and social problems. Yet as in so many similar places on Earth, the people are resilient and hopeful for a more optimistic future. The Nepalese people's religious beliefs help them view their plight with a degree of equanimity, if not acceptance.

Whatever suffering they might experience in this lifetime, they feel it will be made up for in a future life. It is this spirit among many Nepalese that leads visitors to wonder who, in fact, is richer in terms of quality of life. People in rural areas may be facing poverty, malnutrition, disease, unemployment, oppression, civil war, even starvation, yet they approach each day as a gift, grateful for what little they have. The same could certainly not be said for most of the people around you who are so obsessed with achievement and material possessions.

DEAD IN A POOL OF BLOOD

Qualitative research is an enterprise that involves collecting data in the form of observations or interviews with people who are in a position to provide valuable information or stories that advance knowledge of a particular question (Minichiello & Kottler, 2009). It is a methodology that is particularly well-suited to exploring areas that are relatively unknown, or that don't lend themselves to the sort of measurement used in quantitative methods.

One of my (Jeffrey's) doctoral students, Kiran Regmi (mentioned in a previous chapter) was a physician and epidemiologist in Nepal. She not only practiced obstetric medicine—doing surgery and delivering babies—but she also worked for the Ministry of Health studying reproductive health issues. Besides her medical training, Kiran also held master's degrees in anthropology and public health, but she wanted to advance her knowledge of research, especially since she might one day be in charge of health policy for her country.

One of the beautiful things about doing a qualitative study is that you are not only permitted but encouraged to select a research question about which you feel a passionate interest and commitment. For Kiran, a doctor practicing in very remote, isolated regions, she was especially interested in examining why her country had one of the highest maternal mortality rate in the world: more mothers die during childbirth in Nepal than almost anywhere else. This proved especially frustrating and discouraging for Kiran when she would visit a village during her rounds and find a young woman dead in the barn, lying in a pool of blood. In so many cases, Kiran could have saved the mother's life—if only she had been called to the scene or if the mother had been brought to the hospital.

Since she had been trained as a scientist, Kiran was more than a little skeptical about the idea of doing a legitimate research study simply by talking to people. She was used to examining the type of statistical data collected from thousands of cases, extrapolating from this large sample to guide health policy medical decision-making based on these cases. She liked the idea of interviewing new mothers about their childbirth experiences, but she wasn't sure about how to go about this procedure. That is what brought me to Nepal—to help train and supervise Kiran doing qualitative interviews.

Kiran had been trained as a doctor in India, used to asking a series of pointed, "closed" questions of her patients: "Is the pain radiating or centralized?" "Does it hurt more in the morning or the evening?" Doctors are often after simple, one-word answers to their questions, which help them to narrow the diagnostic possibilities. Yet in qualitative research interviews, "open" inquiries are preferred that stimulate people to speak at length about their experiences, perceptions, thoughts, and feelings. Instead of asking a new mother, "Did you have a good experience in the hospital?" essentially leading to particular answer that is not particularly revealing ("yes" or "no"), instead we worked on framing the questions differently: "What was it like for you in the hospital?"

As might be expected of someone who already has three graduate degrees, Kiran was a fast learner; she loved the way that qualitative interviewing elicited such vivid descriptions of childbirth experiences, not to mention that it improved her ability to build better relationships with her patients. It turned out that Kiran's study was truly groundbreaking (see Regmi & Kottler, 2009). It represents the kind of research that really does change the world, a study that not only provided new knowledge about a phenomenon, but also guided changing medical systems to be more responsive.

Much to our mutual dismay, Kiran and I learned that women were dying in childbirth not just because there was a shortage of doctors, but also because the women weren't using the facilities during complicated pregnancies. Based on her interviews, Kiran learned that that the pregnant women weren't actually making the medical decisions; rather, their mothers-in-law were making medical decisions for them. Their husbands' mothers believed that if a daughter-in-law was having a difficult pregnancy or labor, it was because she had done something to anger the gods. Maybe it was best that she die, so that the husband could find a stronger wife.

If that wasn't a disturbing enough finding, we also discovered that the women who did travel to the hospital for care (sometimes walking for several days) had horrific experiences while they were there. They were uneducated and unfamiliar with life in the district city, much less with the workings of a hospital. They were terrified by the strange goings-on within the building, people scurrying back and forth, strange machines making annoying sounds, rude people everywhere. They felt humiliated that men touched their private parts (almost all the doctors except Kiran are men). They were stunned that the staff inserted "snakes" in their arms—nobody explained to them that intravenous tubes provided nourishment. They may have left the hospital with a healthy baby, but also with memories of the experience they would never wish to repeat. This is the report they would bring back to their villages and warn other pregnant women to avoid such indignities.

The results of this study allowed Kiran to make changes in the way obstetric care was provided in her area, involving mothers-in-law in the process, educating staff about how to treat women from the rural villages, and teaching the pregnant women about what to expect. All of this was both interesting and useful, but it was not to become the most important thing that happened during my first visit.

GIRLS DISAPPEARING

Like so many other places in the world, maternal and infant mortality, while tragic, are hardly the only problems they face. Nepal is a country in which the average citizen makes less than $200 per year. During the time of my first visit, there was tremendous political instability and civil war, in addition to the challenges of rampant poverty. Thousands were dying during the insurgency. Thousands more were starving to death or slowly wasting away from malnutrition. We have all seen these images in movies, television, newspapers, and the Internet, but it is something altogether different to see children playing in the streets who you know may never live until puberty.

While following Kiran on her medical rounds through the villages, I heard something about girls disappearing, young girls, some as little as nine years old. I tried to find out more about what this was about.

"What happens to the girls who disappear?" I asked a school principal.

He shrugged. I couldn't tell if that meant he didn't know or didn't want to tell me. I pressed him further. "Where do they go?" I asked again.

"They go away."

"Yes. I understand that. But where do they go?"

"India," he said, and then looked away, trying harder than seemed necessary to organize some things he was carrying in his pocket.

"They go to India?" I repeated.

Nod.

"And what do they do there?"

"Many things."

And so the conversation went for some time, the principal repeatedly changing the subject. Through persistence (he would say rudeness), I eventually learned that girls from the lowest caste, the "untouchables," (lowest of the five castes in the Nepalese system, which has Brahmins at the highest, followed by Chhetri, Vaisya, Sudra, and the outcasts), would often disappear from the village. Other impoverished families of any caste would also "lose" their daughters, all prior to or at puberty.

"But why do they disappear?"

The principal took a deep breath. This was obviously difficult for him to talk about. He explained that after fifth grade, it is necessary to pay fees for children to attend school. Families that were very poor and had multiple children to feed had to make a choice about which ones would remain in school and which would stay at home. Inevitably, the girls were kept at home until such time that they could be married off—or perhaps sold to employers who would find them work in the cities of India.

It turned out that these "employers" were actually sex slavers, and these girls, some as young as 10 years old, would end up in brothels in Bombay. It was never clear to me whether the parents really knew their daughters' fate or not, but perhaps, regardless, they didn't see much choice.

The girls would be taken to brothels in northern India (the border was less than 20 miles away), where they would become sex slaves. There is a belief among some Indian men who are HIV positive that if they have sex with a virgin, it will cure their disease. After the girls become infected and spend a few years as prostitutes, they are released and find their way back to the villages, spreading AIDS throughout the country.

This was just about the most horrifying thing I had ever heard. Nine- and ten-year-old girls being sold as sex slaves? I did a bit of research and learned that more than 7,000 girls each year are abducted or sold into sex slavery in Nepal. Sixty-one percent of the girls are younger than 15, ending up in brothels in Mumbai, India's financial center (McNeil, 2007). One quarter of the girls end up infected with HIV, eventually going back to their home villages where the disease is spread (Silverman, Decker, Gupta, & Maheshwari, 2006). Although this is particularly rampant throughout Nepal because of its pervasive poverty, the U.S. State Department has estimated that more than 150,000 young girls in neighboring countries also end up as prostitutes in India.

All of these statistics and numbers are horrifying, but they are nothing compared to what I experienced next in my conversation with the principal. "You see that one over there?" he said, pointing to a girl of about 15 who was standing with a group of friends at the edge of the school grounds.

"Yes?"

"She will be disappeared next."

"Disappeared? You mean she will be sold?"

"Sold or gone," he said. "It is really quite sad, actually. She is one of the best students in the school, an excellent scholar. But her father is a . . . How do you say? He drinks too much of the alcohol."

"A drunk?"

"Yes, that is so. And her mother has little money. The family does not have much land to grow food. She has brothers, so she must stay at home—until she goes away."

I looked over at the girl and watched her talking to her friends as if this was just another ordinary day in her life, which it was. How many of these days would she have left?

"Her name is Inu," the principal said as he saw me watching the girl.

"I'm just curious about something," I said, trying to make sense of all this, trying to get my head around the idea that girls like Inu are actually traded away because their families can't afford to feed them. Nepal is one of the few countries in the world in which women have a lower life expectancy than men, and one reason for this is because of the oppression they experience.

The principal wagged his head from side to side in the typical Nepalese way of saying yes.

Inu was the first girl sponsored through a scholarship program designed to keep girls in school. She is sitting with Jeffrey (left) and Digumber (right). After five years of support and performing at the highest level, she is currently attending college.

"I'm curious what it costs for someone like Inu to stay in school, I mean, to support her education."

"Well, it is very much, I'm afraid. Too much. There are the school fees of course. Then she must have a spring uniform and one for winter. She needs books and school supplies. It is all very expensive."

"How much?" I repeated, more loudly than I intended.

"More than 3,000 rupees."

"3,000 rupees? That's, like, $50.

"*Hazur*," he responded, meaning agreement.

"Do you mean to tell me that for 3,000 rupees Inu could stay in school for a year?"

The principal was puzzled by slow uptake on this simple math problem, but again he nodded his head from side to side.

Without thinking about what I was doing, without considering the consequences of this impulsive gesture, I reached into my pocked, peeled off three 1,000 rupee notes and handed them to the principal. "Here," I said, "Inu stays in school."

I had no idea where this simple action would lead or how it would change my life in the years to come, but I had to do *something*. What would *you* have done?

GROWING A GENERATION OF WOMEN PROFESSIONALS

I have been cynical much of my life about contributing time and money to charitable causes. They have often seemed to me to be self-serving. Given that the larger ones have 80 percent overhead to cover their expenses, very little of the donations ever get to the host country, and the funds that do arrive are often stolen by unscrupulous politicians. Only a small fraction of the money ever gets to the people in greatest need.

I have traveled a lot in the world and have become used to seeing charity staff and do-gooders riding around in their luxury vehicles and staying at four-star hotels. While in Kathmandu, there was a gathering of charitable groups staying in one of the best hotels, marked by the lineup of Range Rovers and Ford Excursions.

To add to my skepticism, I had seen throughout Nepal the results of charitable efforts—schools built that don't have any supplies or furniture, a cancer hospital that has no drugs to administer chemotherapy, students who have no books. I saw one gorgeous library that had been built by a government, all beautiful hardwoods and expansive views, but the facility had no books at all!

So as much as I wanted to make a difference, I didn't fully trust the large organizations that are frequently profiled in the media. I am not saying that I don't think their work is important, but I wanted to do something on a human scale, on a level in which I could actually *see* a difference. Among all the monetary contributions you may have donated in your life to various causes, imagine actually *seeing* what $50 could do to save a child's life.

My interest in making a difference in people's lives is hardly a recent phenomenon; I have been a teacher and therapist all my adult life. Yet often, one of the eternal frustrations of these helping professions is that we are never quite certain when we've made a difference in people's lives. And even when students or clients do transform themselves, I'm never quite sure what it was that helped most. Maybe it wasn't anything I did or said, but rather some extraneous factor that had nothing to do with me at all.

I remember one client I was seeing in therapy who was saying goodbye with a very happy ending; she was most satisfied with the outcome. I was feeling good about myself, and my work, proud of the progress we had accomplished together. I should have kept my mouth shut but my overconfidence got the better of me. I just had to ask her which, among my so many brilliant interventions, had made the most difference to her. I was reviewing in my mind all the fancy strategies I had employed during our time together—the insightful interpretations, the empathic reflections of her feelings, the complex metaphors I had woven, the inspiring pep talks, the diplomatic and sensitive confrontations. It could be any of them, or all of them, I considered proudly.

When the client pointed to my shoes, again I should have just thanked her and sent her on her way. But I just *had* to know. I had to know what had helped her the most because often in my own life I feel so powerless. I thrive on the feeling that something I've done has been helpful to someone. So I asked her again.

The woman pointed at my shoe once again. "You have a hole on the bottom of your sole," she said.

"So?" I answered, more than a little impatiently.

"Well, all this time we have been talking together I noticed that hole in the bottom of your shoe. You act like such a know-it-all, like you've got everything all together, but you have a hole in your shoe and you don't even know it." Damn it! She even had the audacity to smile at that moment, rubbing it in.

"And your point?"

"It just made me feel better about myself. I mean if you can walk around thinking you're so together and you really aren't, then maybe my problems aren't so bad after all."

Even more striking, this is not an unusual situation. Most of the time we really don't understand how and why change occurs, or what contributes to its lasting effects. Often, the students and clients that I think I've helped the most don't really retain what they've learned or don't practice the concepts after our relationship ends. Just consider how much you have forgotten once a class is over and you move on to the next thing.

The truth is that most changes don't last (Kottler, 2001). So perhaps you can understand why I so hunger to not only make a difference in people's lives, but actually to witness its effects. There are few things that feel better.

If I was going to devote myself to some cause, I wanted to know the efforts were not futile. I wanted to be part of something in which I could see some results in my lifetime, maybe even within months. I wanted to control things in such a way that I *knew* the money was going to the right place and not being swallowed up by waste, expenses, luxuries for staff, and graft. The effort could be modest, on a small scale,—that didn't matter. In fact, small is good. That way I'd have more control over things.

It was then that Kiran and I, with the assistance of another Nepalese friend, Digumber Piya, who worked for Family Planning of Nepal, hatched an audacious idea. If women were dying in Nepal because they felt too shamed to allow male doctors to touch their private parts, what if we grew the next generation of women physicians and health professionals? What if we could get the principals of the local schools to identify young girls who were academically gifted, but also at risk to be sold? What if we could keep them in school as far as their talent and motivation would take them? What if we could mentor them to complete secondary school, then go on to university and graduate school? Just imagine the possibilities of taking a dozen, a hundred, maybe even a thousand marginalized girls and giving them not only a chance at an education but also an opportunity to revolutionize their country?

Initially, Digumber, Kiran, and I funded the program with our own money. We would start with just one girl, Inu, and then build our plans from there. We decided to name the foundation after Kiran's father, Madhav Ghimire, who is the National Poet of Nepal and one of his country's most famous writers. It seemed fitting that our work should honor the life of a man who had written poetry about social justice issues. Furthermore, Ghimire's name was recognized by most educated people of the country, and his portrait hung in many schools.

A FIRST DONOR

When I returned home a few weeks later, I told the students in one of my classes about the project I had begun. It had been an impulsive gesture but was now a decision with far-reaching consequences. I could not make a commitment to a child and her family and then a month, year, or decade later say that I had changed my mind or lost interest. It wasn't just about giving money; it was about making a commitment to sustained, ongoing relationships with the school and community.

I knew that giving money was not nearly enough. Foundations and charities donated money all the time, and often it made little difference. It was through *relationships* that lasting change occurs, or so I have learned through my work as a therapist and teacher.

There was emotion in my voice as I told the story to my students of what I had found in Nepal. I talked about the villages I visited, the beauty of the culture and landscape, and mostly about the girls who so desperately needed help. I became a bit over-passionate, to the point of tears. Embarrassed by my emotional outburst, I sought to make a quick escape as class ended.

"Excuse me, Dr. Kottler?" one student said as she caught me as I started to run. "Can I talk to you?"

At least that is what I think she said to me. Nga is an older Vietnamese woman who is secretly going to school without her family's knowledge or consent. She works three different jobs to support her family, in addition to taking classes in the evenings. From previous conversations—which were always challenging to negotiate, given Nga's strong accent—I had learned that most of her family had been murdered in Saigon during the war. Her boyfriend had been beheaded right in front of her. I knew she had suffered terribly before immigrating to the United States.

"Oh, Nga," I responded, a bit flustered. I didn't have the patience just then to devote the energy it would take to decode her language. "I'm kind of in a hurry right now. Can we talk later?" I assumed that she wanted reassurance after her presentation that night and wanted to talk more about it. It was late at night, almost 9:30. This was my second class back to back, and I was exhausted after working all day.

I saw Nga walking away and felt badly for not being more attentive. Just because I was feeling overwhelmed, that was no excuse to dismiss her. "Wait a second!" I called out to her. "Let's walk out together and we can chat for a minute."

Nga turned to face me with an intense look in her eyes. She reached out and grabbed my hand, pressing a paper into it, as she looked at me. "I want you to give this to the girls of Nepal," she said in a whisper.

"What's that, Nga?" I responded, more out of habit because I was used to asking her to tell me again.

"I say, give this to the children in Nepal," she repeated even more urgently. She pressed the paper more tightly into my hand.

I looked down to see it was money she had given me. "Nga, I can't take this," I protested. "That is so sweet of you, but I can't take your money. I really appreciate . . ."

"You *must* take this. You *must* use this to help the children." There was a fierceness in her voice, a determination in her face, that left little doubt she would not accept no for an answer.

I felt uncomfortable, maybe even embarrassed. I was certainly touched by her gesture, but I was just taken by surprise. I watched Nga walk briskly away and looked down at my hand. Inside, there were two hundred-dollar bills.

I was dumbfounded. This elderly Vietnamese immigrant, struggling in virtual poverty herself, had just given me a huge amount of money with the instructions that I should use it to help the children of Nepal. I had just received my first contribution to the new foundation.

BUILDING A TEAM

During my second visit to Nepal, a year later, I decided to bring a friend and colleague with me. I had been saving money during the previous year, raising a few contributions from friends and family, but keeping plans remarkably modest. Our plan was to expand to support six girls who were all excellent students and highly motivated, but who were from lower-caste families without resources. The girls ranged in age from eight to twelve years old, most from one-parent homes. Since divorce is unknown, the missing parent was often dead of some disease or killed in an accident. This is a country in which the average lifespan is approximately 60 years old, considerably less among the lowest caste in rural areas without access to healthcare.

Saranpur is a village located in the jungle, along the Indian border. It is about an hour's drive from the nearest city along a dirt road, *way* off the beaten track. It is a place that has been virtually forgotten, so we would be among their first foreign visitors.

The whole community turned out, perhaps a hundred children and twice as many adults, all lined up to greet us. As I described earlier, the children formed a gauntlet, two long lines leading from our truck to the entrance of the school. As I walked through the tunnel, each child either placed a string of flowers over my neck or placed flowers in my hands. At the end of the line we walked into the single-room school lined with benches. Parents, grandparents, and children crowded into the dark room. Faces peered in through the windows. We were there to announce to the people the establishment of our scholarship. Each of the six children walked to the front of the schoolroom, accompanied by her parents, to receive the scholarship that would fund her education.

Because Digumber, who would serve as our administrator, worked as a businessman as well as serving on the Board of Family Planning, I knew enough to defer to his expertise about local knowledge. We decided to put into place certain safeguards that ensure that the money contributed would not be squandered. First of all, the money would go directly to the school, rather than to the families; that way we could control expenditures. Secondly, we would spend time in each of the children's homes, have tea with the families, and thereby develop relationships with them over time. Providing scholarships for their education was certainly important, but so was the mentoring we would do, encouraging each child to develop ambitions for the future. Although I would make the trip only once or twice each year, Digumber and Kiran would make frequent visits to check on the children's progress.

As we journeyed through mustard fields, we arrived at each child's residence, consisting of one room enclosed by three walls and a thatched roof. There was a dirt floor, and the back of the house was open to a small plot of land where a few animals might be tethered. Almost all the families maintained a subsistence living, trying to grow enough food to eat.

Our arrival was the biggest thing that had ever happened to this village. The fact that we were there to honor the daughters of the most destitute families may have been perplexing to them, but it also gave status to these girls and their families. It was not enough to provide scholarships unless we could figure out a way that the girls would be allowed, if not encouraged, to continue their education. At each home, Kiran, Digumber, and I gave speeches in front of the neighbors as witnesses, proclaiming our ongoing commitment. It would be far more difficult for the families to pull their girls out of school once this public ritual was completed.

My Spirit is Enriched

The idea of going on this mission was based on everything I believe in most passionately—helping others, providing hope for a better life, feeling a sense of accomplishment. The only problem was that we were going to a place where I felt very frightened and threatened. Everything was different—food, habits, religion, customs, everything. I didn't think I could handle it very well. It all seemed so primitive. Yet my spirit has been so enriched by what I've seen, by the people I've met, by the things I've done. My heart sees clearly what I need to do next and I'm inspired to do what I can. Each smile from a child has been a blessing for me, a reward, that will last me a lifetime. I have changed my mind about what is "primitive." Here, in Nepal, they are so much more advanced than we are back home—especially in relationships. One of my favorite quotes is from Mother Teresa, who worked and lived in this part of the world and who reflected on what she had seen in the supposedly more advanced West: "In the developed countries there is a poverty of intimacy, a poverty of spirit, of loneliness, of lack of love. There is no greater sickness in the world today than that one."

The organization, if we could call it that, was launched. Three people, representing diverse professions and living in different countries, decided to pool our efforts to make a difference with neglected children in a forgotten part of the world. None of us had training or experience in chartable work, much less fundraising. We were all busy with our regular jobs as a physician (Kiran), professor (Jeffrey), and manufacturer (Digumber). We had tried approaching government agencies and philanthropic organizations for support, but we were too small and lacked sufficient resources to be considered. We were on our own and that struck us as being just fine.

Maybe smaller is better. Maybe the efforts of a few people, with a targeted group, and tight control over the resources, is more effective and personally fulfilling. We don't need to change the whole world, or even overhaul the educational structure of a country, to make a significant difference. We can change the world by saving one girl's life. We can select talented, needy children and provide opportunities that will not only transform their lives, but also the lives of all those they will help in the future. We can grow teachers, and nurses, and doctors, and political activists.

But we can do so much more than that—and this is where a central plan for this project (and this book) took on even more intriguing dimensions. It is one thing to go into a part of the world that requires help, assess what needs to be done, and then take steps to provide that assistance. Certainly most of us would like a hand in making such a difference.

What I noticed about my own experiences consulting and volunteering in various regions is that I profit as much as those I help. Each altruistic adventure has transformed me, often in quite unexpected ways. I return from Nepal feeling self-satisfied that maybe I did something that was useful (and how can I really be sure yet what the impact will be?), but I am also reeling from the experience. My view of the world, and of myself, is now different. It is a time to reassess my life priorities, how I spend my time, and my money, what I believe is most important, how I teach, how I love, how I live my life. I am not the same.

Taking a friend along on my expedition, and seeing the children and their families through his eyes, made the journey all that more interesting. It wasn't just a matter of having a companion and partner in this process, but also enjoying the ways that the children we are supposedly helping also influenced us as well.

There is only so much that I, you, or anyone, can do alone. One of the most important, yet challenging, aspects of any effort to promote change is mobilizing the resources of a community. The great anthropologist, Margaret Mead, once famously said, "Never doubt that a small group of thoughtful, committed citizens can change the world; indeed, it's the only thing that ever has." Whatever I could hope to do alone, or with a few friends, is multiplied a hundredfold if I can encourage others to join the effort.

In subsequent chapters, you will hear the stories of dozens of other individuals who have joined our project or launched their own. In each case, they speak not only about the good they have done for others, but also the good they have done for themselves in terms of growth and learning.

Each of us is touched by the lives that we encounter, *if* we remain open to these experiences. Come and meet some of the children and families that we have encountered. As you read their stories, notice what is touched within you.

CHAPTER 4

Stories of Despair and Resilience

We want to tell you about two families, just two examples that represent millions of similar cases all around the world. This book is filled with the stories of those who have volunteered to help, but before we get too deeply into their experiences, we want to first introduce you to a few of the children who are the recipients of such efforts. We want these stories to tug at your heart, to haunt you, to invade your sleep, maybe to make you cry. While we give you only two examples, they stand for all those who are waiting for you to jump in and lend a hand.

A FAMILY

More than half of the women in Nepal are deprived of basic education and healthcare. The problems of illiteracy and poor health are even worse in rural areas of the country, which have been all but neglected by the national government. The current inability of women to make their own decisions regarding their health and welfare has been described as a plight worse than medieval times (Pandey, 2002). Only 11 percent of women in the country are permitted to make their own decisions rather than being controlled by their husbands and fathers (Nepal Ministry of Health, 1998).

Bandipur is a traditional Newari village located on a mountaintop in the foothills of the Himalayas. The Newari people are traditionally farmers and traders, descended from the Mongol tribes of China. They live a communal existence, evidenced in this remote town by a central square that dominates social and commercial activities. Once upon a time, it was situated strategically along one of the main transportation routes between India and Tibet, but a new road bypassing the community was built, leaving it isolated at the end of a one-way road.

There is a small one-room elementary school in the village, along with a high school. Several years ago, an order of Japanese Catholic nuns built a private school that has grown into a campus of connected buildings, but this education costs about five times the average family's total annual income.

Spiraling outward from the central village is a series of pathways that snake over mountain passes into other valleys, where families attempt to scrounge a living growing food on the steep hillsides. In one such hut live Bal Krishna, his wife Parvati Karki, and their three children, twin toddler daughters and a 6-year-old son.

Parvati grew up as an orphan, abandoned by her mother for reasons that she never learned. Because she was illiterate, never having been allowed to attend school, Parvati traveled extensively in search of some employment. She ended up in Mumbai, India where she was helped by an uncle to find work as a cook and housekeeper for wealthy families.

At age 23, Parvati met Bal Krishna, a photographer who proposed marriage. Although she loved this man, she felt that such a match was doomed because she was from a lower caste. She knew she would never be accepted by Bal Krishna's Brahmin-caste family and would always be looked down on as an unsuitable bride.

In spite of her rejections, Bal Krishna continued in his courtship, begging Parvati to marry him. When begging didn't work, he threatened to harm her if she did not agree, and when that did not convince her, he began harming himself and threatening suicide. During one such argument, Bal Krishna banged his head against a stone floor until he knocked himself unconscious. Finally, Parvati relented and agreed to a wedding.

Two years after the couple was married, Parvati gave birth to a boy, followed several years later by twin girls. Eventually they moved to Bandipur, where Bal Krishna's family lived, so they could live on his father's land. Just as Parvati feared, her husband's family refused to accept her; she was invisible to them, even after she became a mother.

Although they lived in the house that Bal Krishna had inherited from his family, it was difficult for the family to survive. Bal Krishna could no longer work as a photographer in such a small town, so they tried to support themselves by growing enough food. To add to their difficulties, Bal Krishna was often sick, sometimes unable to get out of bed. This was a condition that he had tried to hide for some time, because he didn't wish to worry his wife. When she asked him to see a doctor, he said it was just a case of malaria that had to run its course. As his health worsened to the point that he could barely breathe, he concluded that he must have tuberculosis. Since there was no medicine available for either condition, even if they could have afforded it, they had no choice but for the disease to play itself out.

Unfortunately, Bal Krishna continued to deteriorate to the point that he had no choice but to seek medical consultation. He didn't seem very surprised to learn that he had contracted HIV from one of the brothels he frequented when the family had lived in India. This news was devastating to Parvati, however, who not only realized that she would lose her husband, but also felt betrayed in their marriage.

With no financial resources or healthcare available, and Bal Krishna unable to work, Parvati attempted to take care of the children and her dying husband as well as working in the rice fields for a dollar per day. There was a real possibility that they could all starve to death.

Bal Krishna felt both despondent and guilt-ridden for the predicament in which they now found themselves. With no hope, and debilitating depression as well as chronic pain, he believed that the best course of action would be for both his wife and himself to commit suicide. Parvati would have probably agreed to this plan if it weren't for their three children. Bal Krishna was so desperate and miserable that he insisted the children would be better off without them and that his three sisters would care for the children after their death.

Parvati had already sacrificed so much in her life that she was unwilling to surrender to this final humiliation. If her husband wanted to give up and die, that was his choice. She would somehow find a way to continue on her own. Bal Krishna tried to persuade his wife to change her mind, to join him in his death, but she stubbornly refused. They argued constantly about the subject, but by this time he was so weak that he spent most of the time unconscious. A few weeks later, Bal Krishna succumbed to multiple complications from HIV.

Ganga and Jumina from the village of Bandipur, Nepal. Both five-year-old girls are being sponsored with scholarships to support their education.

Parvati was now left alone to support her three children. She had no job, no marketable skills, no education, no family support, no land, and no resources. She had hoped that perhaps her husband's sisters might assist her but they wanted nothing to do with the stigma of this tainted family. They had also never forgiven their brother for marrying a lower-caste woman. To make matters worse, her family became ostracized in the community.

If this seems like the most tragic tale possible, then imagine what could possibly make the situation still worse. One month later, Parvati confirmed her fears as to why she was feeling so sick herself: she was infected with HIV, which she had contracted from her husband.

"I knew then that I would die soon," Parvati said. "Who would look after my children? What would happen to them after I'm gone?" Parvati was so despondent she had no tears left to shed. All she could do was rock back and forth and think about her babies, her children, her wasted life.

Desperate and without any other choices, Parvati wandered the village, hoping that someone might assist her. But there was no one. The children were hungry, at one point going without any food for five straight days. She barely had enough energy to function. It only cost $25 per month to feed her children, but her only source of income (when she wasn't sick) was to pick rice for $1 per day. Many days she could not get out of bed.

To travel from their home to the village and the school, the family has a two-hour walk over two mountain passes in the Himalayas, often in the dark. Each morning, Parvati rises in the dark and gives the children some sweetened tea, and then they make the long trek to the village. Often the children have to support their mother along the trails, since she is experiencing more respiratory problems lately, making it increasingly difficult for her to make the journey. By the time they arrive in the village, dawn has broken, and the children scurry off to school. Parvati rests during the day, reserving her energy for the long walk back to their hut during the cold night.

Kiran and Digumber first heard about Parvati and her plight when she came to the local health clinic for assistance. Kiran, as a physician, could treat some of her physical symptoms, but was also concerned about the family's well-being. Parvati approached Digumber after hearing about our efforts to provide scholarships for needy children who would otherwise be unable to attend school. If ever there was a case crying out for help, this was exactly what we had planned for; Parvati and her children, and so many other families like this one, were the reason we established our foundation in the first place.

When we met with Parvati, her twin daughters, Ganga and Jumina, to let them know that we would pay for them to attend the Catholic boarding school in town, along with their brother, it was heart-wrenching for all of us.

Assured that her children will now have sufficient food, and that they will be able to attend school, Parvati now feels calm and happy. The prospect of impending death no longer frightens her.

FLY OVER THE SKY

Far off the gravel path, down a steep hill, a half-hour's walk from the same village of Bandipur, Geeta's small hut is squeezed into an old wooden house. A space the size of a large closet houses a cluttered kitchen, bedroom, and living room for Geeta, her two younger brothers, and her father, Tilak Bhadur.

The family has no regular source of income because of Tilak's poor health and because his wife (and the children's mother) ran away some years ago, with no warning or explanation. Tilak was well aware that his wife was not happy with him, but he did not know why. He still hopes that one day she will return.

With so little income and almost no resources, Tilak had to pull Geeta, the daughter, out of school. She was a highly motivated and talented student

Geeta has ambitions some day to become a pilot, perhaps the first woman in her country to do so.

with great potential, but Tilak felt he had no choice. He had to find a husband for his 12-year-old daughter, or, if that failed, perhaps give her to a man who claimed he could find her a job in India.

Rituals are an important part of any giving effort, and the more elaborate and public the ceremony, the more meaning it has for the participants. When new girls are offered scholarships, the whole village is called together for a ceremony at the school. All the children are lined up as the primary audience. There is music and dancing, including performances by some of the more talented children. And, of course, there are lots of speeches by all sorts of people who enjoy the spotlight. The village elders take advantage of the gathering to further their political ambitions. The school principal gives a speech about the further needs of the school. Sometimes a random person stands up and grabs the microphone, glad for the opportunity to rail about one thing or another. We give speeches talking about our vision of the future and our plans to help all the children in the school. Finally, the scholarship girls are asked to say something about what they want to do when they complete their education.

After Geeta was awarded a scholarship by the Foundation, she was asked in front of her village what she wants to do when she graduates from school some day. Most of the time when girls are asked this question, they either mention being a teacher or a nurse since these are the only two professions that they have heard of that are suitable for a woman. Beside Kiran, they have never seen a woman do anything else, nor have they ever heard that women were *allowed* to do other jobs.

It was all the more surprising when Geeta hesitated before answering the question in front of a crowd of her peers. She was obviously embarrassed about something. Finally, she looked up and pointed at the sky.

What did that mean? What was she pointing to?

After some back and forth with our translator, he finally said with a smile, "Fly. She wants to fly a plane."

"She wants to be a pilot?"

"Yes, that's it, a pilot. She wants to fly airplanes in the sky."

This was certainly an unusual career goal for a girl in a country in which there may not have been a single female pilot. What could she possibly be thinking and where did this unusual idea come from?

"Geeta," we asked gently so as to not embarrass her further. "Have you ever seen an airplane before?"

She nodded solemnly. "Yes, one time I saw one fly over our village." She pointed to the sky once again as if tracking its trail across the horizon.

When questioned further, Geeta disclosed through tears that she hoped by flying in the sky she might be closer to her mother, who had abandoned her long ago.

A postscript: As this book was going to press, we just learned that Geeta, at age 14, disappeared from the village. As best we understand it, she may have eloped with a 15-year-old boy who came to the village as a porter, working on a bus to load luggage.

This child's father was killed by a tiger, leaving the family destitute and without any means to survive, even on a subsistence level. The mother disfigured her face in her grief, making certain she could never remarry. This girl was provided a scholarship so she could remain in school and continue her education.

STORIES OF IMPACT

Both Geeta and Inu's stories bring a closer view of who you are actually helping when you decide to volunteer your time on behalf of some social justice project. Whether you work in the inner city of your own community, at a woman's shelter, hospice, homeless shelter, substance abuse facility, or go abroad to spend time in another culture, the stories of the people you help will stay with you throughout your lifetime. Whatever else you decide to do with your life, whether in business, politics, science, education, the arts, or any other profession or job, you remain connected to those you help as long as you remember them.

DIFFERENT PATHS TO THE SAME PLACE

Whereas Jeffrey's efforts have been centered primarily on work with children in Nepal, Mike's path has taken a different trajectory altogether. When he graduated from college several years ago, he was lost, without any particular plans except to get together with some friends to see something of the country before he joined the rat race. Like Jeffrey, little did he know what this cross-country trip would become for him.

In the chapters within the next section of the book, beginning with Mike's story, you will hear about the impact that volunteer and social justice efforts have, not just on the recipients, but by those who give of themselves.

PART II

Stories of Impact

CHAPTER 5

Road Trip

Mike's commitment to the transformative power of travel and social justice issues began just as college was ending. He had no clue what he wanted to do with his life. Along with two friends from school, he began an odyssey across the country in an old, broken-down RV, stopping along the way to talk with people who had defined their own paths in life. Six years and thousands of miles later, their initial journey has turned into Roadtrip Nation, a grassroots movement that has linkages to over 350 universities around the country and is a nationally syndicated television series on PBS.

At 29 years of age, Mike had visited all 48 continental states, as well as several countries, taking college students on sojourns along back roads, exposing them to the world outside of their campuses. Most of these students had never traveled much before, nor had they had much exposure to the spontaneity of life on the road. Their experiences were carefully documented through many documentary series and in several books (Gebhard, Marriner, & Gordon, 2003; Marriner, McAllister, Gebhard, & Bollinger, 2005).

A little more than a year ago, Mike had spent another long day on the road, pulling into New York City in an ancient RV, longing for a solid night's rest without having to worry about shepherding the students on their next adventure. As he lay his head down, the phone rang. "Must be someone from the West Coast," he thought immediately since it was past midnight.

Indeed, it was a new friend calling from California, a girl he'd met in a coffee shop just a few weeks earlier. "Hey Mike, I told you I'm going to Nepal with a group of people. Why don't you come with me?"

Granted, Mike was in the middle of a summer fling with this girl, but he was also hungry for new experiences. The last decade of his life had been about expressing his spontaneity, following his whims, exploring what's just beyond the next horizon and the one after that. As productive as he'd been, building an organization from scratch, he was also hungry for something new, something different. He'd yet to experience that sense of purpose that comes from helping those who need it the most. This seemed like a perfect opportunity to keep pushing that envelope, so naturally he agreed to go with her.

PART 1 — TAKING OFF

The Backstory

I (Mike) remember the second semester of my senior year really well. I had that feeling of impending doom associated with not knowing what the heck you want to do with your life. Four years at school was supposed to help me figure that out, right?

Biology was a wonderful major that taught me how to think, but the deeper I got into my studies, the less I could picture myself wearing a lab coat or doctor's garb to work every day. In fact, the sheer thought of it made me sick. But what was I supposed to do—throw my education down the drain? I decided to ride it out, get my degree, and figure things out from there.

In life it seems like there are four main stages: childhood, adolescence, adulthood, and old age. On the day I graduated from college, I decided to create my own fifth stage and insert it right between adolescence and adulthood. I decided to call it "odyssey."

A few of my buddies—Nathan, Brian, and Amanda—were going through their own life crises, so we decided to join forces and create our own adventure in the form of a cross-country road trip. Our idea was to drive across the country for several months and meet with people from all walks of life to learn how they got where they are today. As college graduates, we already had some idea about how to be lawyers, doctors, and accountants, but what about all the other possibilities?

A few months into planning our trip, we were making sandwiches at Brian's parents' house when we heard his parents talking about their future

It doesn't take much to launch new adventures. In this case, our intrepid heroes bought an old, beat-up recreational vehicle, repainted and fixed it up as best they could, and then headed out on the open road. It isn't a lack of money or resources that stops most students from traveling, but rather a failure to make traveling a priority.

plans for the old family motorhome. They were planning on donating it to a charity, but we convinced them to sell it to us for a few thousand dollars. Sure, it was old and rundown, but it seemed to us like a big beautiful beast that would become our new home. It would just need a little work to fix it up, especially the rather geriatric brown color of the vehicle. We found neon green paint on sale at the hardware store for the fantastic price of $3.25 per gallon—an incredible bargain, you have to admit. We bought them out of stock and proceeded with our RV makeover. By the time we were done, we were the proud owners of a bright green RV with a nice clean, blue stripe down the side. To our dismay, the racing stripe didn't help with the velocity of the vehicle, which maxed out at 55 MPH.

For months, we planned our route across the country, researched people we could meet along the way, deferred as many student loans as we could, and applied for as many credit cards as possible to fund our journey. Finally, the day arrived for our great departure. Our journey would route us along a 15,000-mile figure eight, stretched far out across America. We would begin in San Francisco, go east through the barren Nevada desert, into the welcoming Nebraska and Iowa cornfields, north into Pennsylvania, Vermont, New Hampshire, Maine and the rest of quaint New England. We'd head down through the buzzing epicenters of Boston, New York, and Washington, DC. Venture south through slow-paced Virginia, the Carolinas, and Georgia. Turn west at Biloxi, Mississippi, drive through crazy New Orleans, into Texas, and then turn north into Oklahoma, driving through Colorado and magnificent Wyoming. In Wyoming, we spun west again, heading into the great mountains of Montana, through northern Idaho, and into the Pacific Northwest. From Seattle, we began our descent home through Oregon, and then finally back to California.

The journey would take us three months and had slowly transformed our view of the world and our role in it. We began to believe that we really could seek out our own paths in life and not get stuck in the lives our college degrees had prepared us for. That cliché "follow your passion" seems so lofty and distant, but after that trip, we realized that the ideal was actually attainable.

We met a lobsterman in Maine who had jettisoned a nine-to-five corporate existence for a life on the water. "Once the sea gets in your blood, it's impossible to get it out," Manny told us. He didn't live in a glamorous loft or drive a fancy car, but he had no one else to answer to but himself. And he got to spend his days around his passion, the sea.

Over the course of our travels we met many others like Manny who defined our journey. We met the head of programming at the Cartoon Network, whose passion was watching TV as a kid. We met the founder of Nantucket Nectars, who graduated from Brown University and moved to Nantucket Island to start a business with some of his friends around their passion for the juices that they had discovered in Spain: "When I told my parents of my plans to not go to law school and to start this business, they thought I was crazy. They were, like, 'who starts a juice company?'"

One of our most memorable interactions was with a man in northern Vermont named Michael Jagger. He started his own independent design agency that worked with Burton Snowboards to launch the snowboarding revolution back in the 1980s. He told us, "When you magnify what it is you believe in, the world will conspire to support you on that path."

Mechanics in Texas, environmental activists in Washington, D.C., brewers in Seattle, shoe designers in Oregon, filmmakers in New York, symphony conductors in Boston—the people we encountered were varied and eclectic, and the only common theme that connected them was their determination to define their own paths in life. We found this so interesting and inspiring that we couldn't stop the journey, and continued long past our original schedule.

Taking Off for Nepal

> "And we swing west. Usually, almost always, I find myself swinging east when I leave home. But this time, we head into the west. Waaaaayyyyy west. Further west than I could even imagine. So west that we're going into the East. Not a bad way to spend Christmas Eve."

—Nepal Journal entry #1, December 24, 2006

The 17-hour plane ride to Asia provided plenty of time for reflection. Much of my 20s had been built on impulse, but this latest scheme seemed pretty extreme, *way* out of my comfort zone. I'd traveled America extensively, but my international travel experience was surprisingly slim. This would be my first extended trip over the Pacific, to Asia, further off the grid than I had ever been before.

We had a day layover in Bangkok to try and ditch the jet lag before heading up into the mountains of Nepal. That day was surreal. No matter how much of Asia I had seen on TV or read about in the papers, nothing could have prepared me for experiencing firsthand the racecar pace, putrid smells, steamy weather, telephone wires wrapped like birds nests, and damp slums linked together by small alleys with ferocious motorbike racers blurring the lines between "walkway" and "street."

I spent the day on a basic walkabout, traveling mostly by alley to avoid the motorbikes. At the end of one alley, I came across a Muslim mosque that most tourists clearly avoided. The men and children here were some of the most peaceful I had encountered in my brief stay. Much of Bangkok seemed like a rapid flurry of neon lights, chaotic freeways, and loud-speaking locals. Maybe it was the jet-lag, but it was an intense, cultural introduction to life in Asia. For all the news media I had absorbed in the United States about how threatening Muslim people were, I was shocked to find that my experience was exactly the opposite—there were more smiles and open arms in the Muslim neighborhood than I had experienced along my entire walkabout that day.

Down the alley from the Muslim neighborhood was clearly some sort of Buddhist area. There was a series of raised wooden structures with monks praying inside and orange robes draped out the back. It was a little raised and disconnected from the street, so that it felt a bit inaccessible, but there was something so beautiful about the area that I almost didn't even want to interact with it. I didn't want to disturb the monks, just to absorb all the peacefulness they were emitting.

This slummy, beautiful mix of culture was no more than seven blocks from our swanky hotel. I couldn't help but think about all the people back at the hotel, sitting by the pool, sipping tropical drinks, totally disconnected from the rest of the world—which happened to be right in their backyard.

On my way back to the hotel, I came across a small, makeshift café in the bottom of a local family's apartment. They served many things, but the only thing that stood out was Tiger Beer. There were two fold-out tables placed in the alley where customers could enjoy their purchase, and one was already taken up by a group of young policemen, probably about my age. My experience on the road in the middle of America (which wasn't too much more foreign than this) had taught me the unspoken rule of pub tourism—buy a round for the locals.

The young cops certainly took my beer offering, but they didn't exactly warm up right away. They made it very clear that they "hated" my President, and until proven otherwise, assumed I was part of his "regime." After we bonded in our shared repugnance for America's current foreign policy, things started to warm. They ordered local dishes of octopus and dog legs for the table, I politely tried to indulge, and we opened up a very spirited conversation about American football and Tom Brady, their favorite NFL quarterback. I realized that these guys weren't that different from me. I felt strangely connected to these new friends sitting on the other end of the table, more than I would have ever anticipated.

The next morning, my jet lag (and hangover) began to subside as we made our way back to the Bangkok airport. Boarding the plane to Kathmandu was a little different than boarding the plane to Bangkok, a very developed city with an international airport that actually rivaled LAX. On the other hand, Kathmandu Airport, the largest airport in Nepal, was something that I could have never even imagined.

PART 2—DIVING IN

The Backstory

Coming home from our road trip across America was certainly the most difficult part of the journey. On the road we had long exhausting days with frequent, desolate breakdowns and long, cold, sleepless nights—but nothing could have prepared us for the pressure once we returned.

We heard comments from our parents and friends such as "So, now that your road trip is over, what are you going to do with your life?" It would have been a lot easier just to drift back into college-mode and get some kind of decent-paying corporate job, or start applying to grad schools, just to get everyone off my back. But I just couldn't do it. After listening to the stories from all of these people who had set out on their own and truly built lives around their passions, I would have been a huge hypocrite if I just jumped back on that path without even trying to find my own way. In some ways, the road trip had been a curse; it showed me how it was possible to actually follow my passion, and now that I knew that, there was no turning back.

Even though I still didn't know what I wanted to do with my life, one person's advice was still ringing in my head. A business start-up guru from San Francisco told me, "Even if you don't know what you want to do with your life, just engage in what truly motivates you now." When I thought about it, what truly motivated me most was the road trip I had just taken. Friends would come over to Nathan's house and watch hours and hours of video footage we had taken on our trip. It turned out that lots of other people, beside us, were also trying to find their roads in life.

Someone we had met on the road knew a writer from *Forbes* magazine. They discussed our adventure, and the writer ended up wanting to do a story on us. That article, released about six months after we got home from our trip, lead to a publishing contract with Random House. When they heard we had all of our interviews and experiences on tape, they felt it would make an interesting book. That was great news to us; not only did the signing bonus help us get out of debt (we had racked up $30,000 on several credit cards to fund the trip), but the book gave us a broader way to share the experience.

We spent the next two years transcribing the interviews, writing the book, and learning how to edit so we could compile the video footage into a very rough independent documentary. I wasn't making any money from the project, just basically living hand-to-mouth trying to buy time and continue doing what I loved. By this point, many of my friends from college were now successfully working for consulting firms as bankers or real estate agents. They were making great progress by society's standards, and yet I was basically homeless, living day-to-day out of a green bus.

Diving In to Nepal

"What an interesting adventure. What the hell lay in front of me? I have no freaking idea. All I can really observe at this point is myself—what am I the most curious about? What am I the most excited for? It's definitely the people. Why does everyone keep telling me that people in the third world are some of the happiest people in the world, even amidst all of their poverty? What do their Christmas mornings look like? If these people had our lives in the west, and more presents under the tree, would they truly be any happier?"

—*Nepal Journal entry #2, December 26, 2006*

Kathmandu. I caught my first glimpse of the Himalayas during our descent into the airport. Huge, magnificent peaks that seemed so high I thought my eyes were playing tricks on me. That brief moment of peaceful tranquility lasted for the first part of the descent, until we got closer and I could really see what we were getting ourselves into. Flimsy buildings sandwiched together so closely it looked like if I leaned on them they would fall over. Winding dirt roads with oceans of cars, buses, bikers, and pedestrians all crawling on top of each other like ants eating a cupcake. At first it was intriguing, right up until we realized we would soon be a part of the frenzy.

The airport did not disappoint. Old, Russian, Cold War–style bomber planes littered the runway. Walking by them, you could tell they had been originally designed for the military, but now that the Cold War was over they had been refurbished for Nepal's small, flimsy airlines, such as Buddha Air and Yeti Airlines.

Once we got to the terminal and grabbed our bags, the real fun began. When you try to get a cab in New York or most major cities in America, it's certainly a struggle, but in Kathmandu it's all-out war—not because you're fighting for a cab, but because all the cabbies are fighting for *you*. Taking the bus into town was surreal. It made the slums of Bangkok feel like Disneyland. But for as much apprehension as I immediately felt getting off the plane, as soon as we eased into Katmandu life, everything felt remarkably safe. If someone had shown me in advance a picture back home of the hotel we would be staying in, or the neighborhood we would frequent, I don't know if I would have hopped on that plane on Christmas Eve back at Los Angeles Airport. But now that I was here, everything felt remarkably peaceful. I swear, if I had dropped a dollar on the street, someone would have picked it up and given it back to me. And as poor as these people are, they seemed remarkably happy.

Before I came to Nepal, a friend of mine had gone to South America as part of a similar small aid effort. He told me that even though the people had nothing, they were just as happy, if not more, than the average person back home. For some reason that really stuck with me, I just couldn't believe that

that would be true. How could you really be happy with nothing—basically living in dirt, breathing this brown air, and swimming through this mess of a city on a daily basis? But he was right. The people here were unbelievably peaceful. Kids weren't playing in the streets with their new remote-controlled car, they were out working with their parents to put food on the table, but they were still completely open, kind, and gracious. I couldn't help but think that the material "stuff" that is the focus of our lives back home only gets in the way of achieving that sense of peace and fulfillment that so many of these people had.

Nepalese people have amazing faith. Faith they won't get hit by a car driving down these crazy streets. Faith that they'll find food to put on the table. Faith that there are powerful spiritual forces greater than themselves. And the funny thing is that after being here for just a few days, I have not seen one car accident, have not seen one person get hit. Perhaps there is some connection between faith and fate. Faith and happiness. That almost creates a sort of self-fulfilling prophecy . . . to some degree at least. What a beautiful culture this is. There is so much more here than just "faith in God." There is Faith in Life.

—Nepal Journal entry #3, December 28, 2006

After a few days in Kathmandu, our work with the Madhav Ghimire Foundation would begin. We needed to go deeper into Nepal, which would require another plane flight into the southwest part of the country. Taking the bus back to the Kathmandu airport, we boarded a puddle-jumper plane, prayed to whatever Nepalese god would listen for a safe flight, and ventured to a small town in Chitwan, which was located even further off the grid.

PART 3—IN OVER MY HEAD

Backstory

When the book about our road trip experiences had taken off and the documentary aired on PBS, we were 25-years-old and at a place in life we could have never predicted even 24 months prior. Heck, I was a biology major, and here I was writing a book and producing a documentary for PBS. Wasn't I supposed to be in a laboratory or something? It was surreal.

While I was on the road doing the promotional book tour, I began speaking at a lot of college campuses to screen the film and share our experiences from the road. The footage and those experiences were certainly having an impact, but it became apparent that these students needed to hit the road for themselves instead of merely enjoying our adventures vicariously.

I'd heard of something called "the gap year" in Australia, New Zealand, and parts of Europe; students from all over the world take a year off between high school and college, or college and work, to travel the world and discover their path. I wondered why more of us don't do that in America, and why we have all that pressure to shift so urgently and aggressively from one phase in life to another before we have even figured out where we want to go.

A larger vision for Roadtrip Nation began to emerge, one that was based more on facilitating students to hit the road on their own, rather than simply experiencing *our* roadtrip. I had no interest in becoming the "spokesmen for our generation," as agents, Hollywood producers, and talk show hosts wanted to label us. I didn't want to just talk about what I had done, especially the experiences that were over, but rather I wanted to become a vehicle for others to share similar adventures.

In Over My Head in Nepal

The airport in this district town, if you could even call it that, resembled a humble, dusty bus depot more than an actual airfield. But by now my travel senses were a bit more heightened, and what had made me feel apprehensive in Bangkok now enlivened me in Chitwan.

Our first task, so to speak, was to visit a local college to give a few presentations to the faculty and some of the students. There was also a banquet to honor the first girl who had ever received a scholarship from the foundation. Where would she have ended up if it wasn't for receiving that scholarship? The alternatives seemed horrific, but here she was, standing in front of this audience, just about to graduate high school and getting ready to enter college. Her dream was to one day be a professor like Jeffrey, and she was actually on the road to doing it. It blew my mind that by sponsoring this girl, giving her $50 each year to cover schooling costs, actually saved her life. I thought to myself, "How can that be possible? $50 gets you a night out on the town. But here, in the mountains of Nepal, it saves little girls' lives?" My parents gave me $300 that Christmas to buy a new surfboard, but there was no way I could spend that on a board after seeing what that money could do here. It's one thing to see it on a UNICEF box in line at the market, but when you are out there, feeling these stories directly, the power is suddenly very real.

We continued deeper into rural Nepal by bus, visiting a local village that the foundation had sponsored. As soon as the bus rolled up it felt like a riot. Hundreds of villagers swarmed around the bus, with smiles bigger than any American kid would have on Christmas morning. Getting off the bus felt like being in the middle of a parade. I felt a bit guilty; I hadn't even done anything yet! But it was beautiful to see how deeply the foundation had affected these people's lives. It had saved their little girls, kept them in school, and given them a future. And by giving their children something to hope for, it gave the entire village something to dream about. It hit me that simply "dreaming" is such a huge part of life. If you don't have hope, what is there to live for? All these people needed was a little help, a little bit of hope, to jump-start their lives. Those dreams came in the form of sponsoring several of their girls, but the impact spread village-wide.

That afternoon, once things settled down, we had a ceremony in the center of the village where existing scholarship recipients were praised for their work, and new girls' scholarships were awarded. The Red Sox winning the World Series in 2005 doesn't even compare to the reaction of these girls.

Leaving the village, we continued our journey further into the Himalayas, through some of the most remote country I had ever seen. We arrived at a village high on a mountaintop with the most breathtaking views of the Annapurna mountain range spanning the horizon. They rose up from the valley floor to stretch beyond the clouds at over 25,000 feet.

The Nepalese administrator of the foundation, Digumber Piya, had been born in this village. He was a successful entrepreneur who had made a name for himself and was now committed to giving back to the village from where he had come—including building a new school for the same teachers who had taught him when he was growing up. He was a sincere guy, with a big laugh, who had that swelling heart associated with living amidst these people's hardships day-to-day. When he walked into that village, he was treated like a king.

We were also joined in Bandipur by Dr. Kiran Regmi, the third member of the foundation team. Whereas Jeffrey does most of the fundraising, Kiran and Digumber work with the students, conduct home visits, and determine which families are most in need of scholarship assistance.

Kiran was fantastic. A former student of Jeffrey's, she grew up in Nepal and went on to get several advanced degrees in medicine, anthropology, and public health. She even went on to do research at Harvard, which begged the question, "What is she doing living in Nepal?" She could be living in Cambridge, making a boatload of money, but instead she chose to come back to her home. One of only a handful of woman physicians in her country, she sees patients mostly out of her home and has to dry X-ray film by hanging it on a clothesline in the backyard. She had a regal but tired sense about her, a woman who is equipped with talent and schooling *and* actually gives a damn. She is a powerful woman whose life backs up her ideals, and it made me wonder if I could ever do the same.

PART 4 — NEW VISTAS

The Backstory

Our agency continued to set up meetings with heads of various TV stations. The president of MTV wanted to do a *Roadtrip Nation* series, but when it got funneled down to her program development department, they started changing the idea way too much. They would insist, "We want you to go interview CEOs of major corporations and see what kinds of cars they drive and how big their houses are." It was so far from our original vision that we felt dispirited.

Many organizations reach a point on the verge of success in which they have to choose whether to "sell out" their vision to satisfy the media and corporate masters, but we were unwilling to do that. Instead, we went underground for a few years to build our own independent organization, Roadtrip Nation, within the aesthetic we had originally envisioned. First, we began forging partnerships with a handful of college campuses across the country by starting an educational program called "Behind the Wheel." Students would apply to this program through their career center, in teams of three, for the chance to hit the road in our RV and interview people from all across the country.

Our first student team was from New York University. Randy, Ryan, and Mike were three friends who, much like us in that first year after college, were trying to find their paths in life. They built their own itinerary, booked their interviews, and hit the road after graduation in our old green RV. Along the way, they met with anyone from the guy who produced Nirvana's first album to a Pulitzer Prize-winning novelist. Their experience showed us that other students in our generation could realize just as powerful an impact from this experience as we had when we first hit the road.

Brian and I went along with the NYU team to film their journey. We acted as a pseudo-camera team for the trip, even though we had no real film experience; we were completely making it up as we went. We had no production budget or staff. It was just the semi-blind leading the blind, on the road again, charging it on our credit cards, trying to make something happen. Once we finished filming the trip, Nathan began to edit together the eight-part documentary series (by himself, on his parents' kitchen table), and I began to call up local PBS stations to see if they would air the series that Nathan was editing. Many of them had already broadcast our first documentary, so we thought we had a good chance of having them pick up our new series.

Once the series was picked up by public television around the country, we were able to raise some funds to build an organization to help fuel the future of *Roadtrip Nation* so we could stop going into debt. Everything felt like it was coming together. Not only were we thoroughly engaged in a path we were extremely passionate about, but we were doing it on our own terms and maintaining the authenticity we had started with. I originally hit the road to try and figure out what to do with my life, and now that journey had actually turned into my career, such as it was.

New Vistas in Nepal

"How do I even explain these mountains? So much energy . . . everything seems to break down and then recuperate on such a higher, more dramatic level. Joy, adventure, empathy, understanding, creativity, appreciation, clarity, belief . . . you get lifted up quicker and broken down easier. And you get put back together in ways you could have never imagined."

—*Nepal Journal entry #5, January 8, 2007*

After our work in Bandipur had ended, it was time to go even further into the mountains. Six months prior, there would have been no way I could have imagined spending my Christmas vacation going so deeply into the Himalayas for aid-work that we would actually have to go by foot, because the land was too desolate for roads. But that, in fact, was actually the situation I happily found myself in now.

I had driven all across America throughout my 20s, but all of that domestic travel paled in comparison to these mountains and everything that lay within them. As we began our ascent, on foot, into the Annapurna mountain range, it struck me how comfortable I had become with all of this. What began as terrifying was now exhilarating. I recognized the changes that were happening in my consciousness, tried to understand them, and then found new experiences to dive in further.

Day after day we saw new vistas and visited beautiful villages that were way off the beaten path. There were no tourist shops or local cafes on those streets. There wasn't even electricity and everything that accompanies it—phones,

It is not only the people you meet along the way that can influence and impact you, but also the power of the land. This mountain of Macchapucchare (Fish Tail) has never been successfully climbed. It served as a beacon for members of our team throughout our exploration of this region.

lights, heaters. These people were living way out there, several days walk from any kind of civilization.

The further out we got, the more we could see how ancient and museum-like the culture really was. So many of the things we take for granted in the west were major life-changing factors out here. Forget about having a car to drive to a hospital—these people had to create their own thread and then begin to make their clothes. They made concrete by breaking boulders into stones and then used hammers to pound the rocks into powder, mixed with water. They did their laundry in streams. There was no general store with basic goods for survival—everything had to be made from scratch by the villagers.

It was beautiful to see that kind of living, but also disgusting when you began to consider all the stupid crap we worry about back home, like what to wear to the movies, how to get the best tan, or what *type* of food to eat for dinner. In the Annapurnas, they worry about having enough layers to survive the long Himalayan winter, keeping enough wood (or yak dung) in the stove to stay warm at night, or finding enough food just to keep the family fed.

Being out there, walking among those huge, humbling mountains, and trying to help people who were living such a different existence than I was used to back home truly began to change me. We had only been in Nepal for a few weeks, but the impact of those weeks rivaled all my experiences during my 20s on the road in America.

Part 5—Taking it Home

The Backstory

Once our first student-based documentary series had been broadcast on 50 PBS stations across the country, and some funding came in the door from different organizations, things really started to take off. Appearances on national talk shows, book launches, media interviews, all contributed to the buzz. I was still just a vagabond, living in my parents' garage, trying to save enough money to make ends meet, and yet my "job" involved talking to some of the most powerful and wealthy people in the country. It was crazy and more than a little unreal. I never took much of it very seriously, because I wasn't sure when the ride would end.

Roadtrip Nation began to grow as our partnership with public television and several sponsors solidified. We had been able to fund more than 200 students to hit the road, many of whom had never traveled much prior to that experience. We expanded our affiliations to more than 350 universities across America. For so many years, we had been working out of a garage, or our old green RV, but now we moved into a big warehouse that we converted into our headquarters. We hired a staff of dozens to help with the production, editing, and logistics of running a worldwide organization.

Sometimes I wonder where I would be if I hadn't decided to hit the road with Nathan and Brian when we got out of college. Would I be working in a lab somewhere? Would I be a rich businessman? Would I have gone on to law school, medical school, or some other traditional route? When I think about that, I try to remind myself that it's impossible to look back in time, or to look forward into the future, and truly figure out what any of us should do with our lives. What I've learned from spending so many years on the road is that everyone is out there searching, trying to find their way. The most important thing is always staying close to what matters most. It may be different for everyone, but just as Michael Jagger told us on the first road trip, "When you magnify what it is you believe in, the world will conspire to support you along that path."

Taking it Home from Nepal

> "I'm just beginning to comprehend all of this, but how can I really? We're just
> another group of stupid American tourists, worlds apart from these people,
> coming to take photos of the mountains to hang as "Trophies of the Unknown"
> on our mantels once we get back home. But can this be something more?
> Can I actually take these experiences home? Can they change me?"
>
> *—Nepal Journal entry #8, January 14, 2007*

We had spent days walking out of the Annapurnas, trying to get to the point where roads began to emerge. After all the time we had spent on the mountain with the villagers, insulated in our band of merry trekkers away from general civilization, it was weird even to see a dirt road again. Once we got to the first main village where we were supposed to catch a ride, part of me almost didn't want to leave. I certainly wanted a shower, but I had become so connected with being disconnected from the rest of the world that it was hard to reattach.

On the ride down the mountain, most of my mental reflection was just trying to grasp how awesome the experience had been. But when we got on the bus to the first airport, then onto the puddle jumper flight to Kathmandu, then to Bangkok, and then onward to the long flight back to LAX, things really began to sink in.

My life until that point had been about finding myself. I'd learned how to unplug from the rest of society, hit the road, explore the world for myself, and define my own path based on my passion. What I learned in Nepal is that that's not enough. There's more to life than trying to find yourself, and paving your own road. Certainly that is a critical step, a crucial part of the process, because if I hadn't figured that out I wouldn't have even been in Nepal in the first place. I would have been locked into some path that had no reflection of what I believe in, stand for, or love most. But the journey does not end there.

I learned that my path had to keep going in the direction of helping others. The question now became "How do I use this road I have discovered to actually make a difference in the lives of others?" Like Kirin, Digumber, and Jeffrey, I wondered if I had the courage to do that. And I wondered what difference I could make, or what level of difference, and what compromises I was willing to make.

When I returned home, I got back into my normal routine; we had another television series to produce, more colleges picking up our educational programs, and more employees joining the team to help us make *Roadtrip Nation* happen. Things were moving and I had a responsibility to keep the ship sailing smoothly ahead. But now I became focused on how we could make *Roadtrip Nation* more socially relevant. How could we make a bigger difference in the world than just producing our television series? I believe that we'd already done some good work for our generation, but there could be so much more.

Now that I had experienced firsthand the wonders of international travel, the next logical step was to take our organization to a larger scale. We began launching trips for students in Australia, Poland, Argentina, Trinidad. France, Brazil, Uganda, New Zealand and other far-off places, and the feedback from the students was amazing. Not only were they discovering their roads in life, but they were becoming citizens of the world, more globally conscious, and connected with issues that exist beyond America's borders.

We also took a harder look at *Roadtrip Nation* domestically and began to wonder how we could inspire students from disadvantaged households to go to college and create their own dreams for their lives. We began to realize that the children of Nepal are not the only ones in need of help, and that there was a lot that *Roadtrip Nation* could do here in America to make a difference.

I had made plans to return to Nepal for the next installment, but while training for the rigorous demands of mountain travel, I injured my back and had to remain behind. This was absolutely devastating, since I was the one who was supposed to do the principal filming of the trip to document the experiences of the students. I was left to dream about next year, which was all the more difficult because I hate living in the future.

I returned to Nepal in 2009 and continue the work there. I may not have the time and space in my life to make this my full-time focus, but I spend as much time as I can on it, knowing how much difference I can make with the little work that I do.

Sometimes I think about the work that Kiran is doing in her doctor's office every day in Nepal, how she is battling against all the odds to help her people, knowing that at any moment, she could leave and have a very different life somewhere else. I think about the ways that Digumber devotes much of his time and resources to helping those who are most in need. I see the direction that Jeffrey's life is taking toward devoting more commitment to his work abroad. I wonder if I am doing enough?

Then I remember that you can't define your path in life based on comparisons to other people, and that my own calling had its own impact on the world. Jessica Mayberry, the founder of Video Volunteers (profiled in Chapter 12), has a favorite quote that sums this up perfectly: "Don't ask what the world needs. Ask what makes you come alive and go do that. Because what the world needs is people who have come alive."

CHAPTER 6

Being Lost

Often, adversity, trials, and tribulation bring about unprecedented growth. Almost all efforts to help people in underdeveloped countries or communities take place in a context of minimum comforts, bewildering cultural differences, and often many hardships that can be both physically taxing and psychologically challenging.

The tales of adventure and accomplishment that people bring back from faraway places sound romantic and exciting. The amusing, interesting stories instill in listeners feelings of envy that they had not been there for all the fun and adventure. Often, however, such narratives leave out the difficult and trying times that were endured to achieve the desired results.

In most stories of travel experiences that produce indelible memories, there are embedded (or hidden) aspects of extreme discomfort and challenging situations, even a certain amount of pain (Kottler, 1997; Rapoport & Castenera, 1994). Such experiences are similar to childbirth, in the sense that the memorable events are often accompanied by excruciating agony, which is forgotten soon after the child is born. So it is with many helping efforts, especially those in foreign cultures; you often feel lost and *way* out of your element. Sometimes this experience of being lost is quite literal, as this following story illustrates.

JEFFREY: WE LOST A MEMBER OF OUR TEAM

Kristine was a bright, energetic, yet somewhat quiet member of our team. She preferred to keep to herself mostly, spending her idle time reading Asian history

These are all the preschool-age children in the village of Siklis, a remote Gurung village in the Annapurna Himalaya range.

books or walking at her own pace. As a scholar of Asian colonial history, she had more than a passing interest in the politics and traditions of this part of the world. She was a new faculty member at our university, still adjusting to life after graduate school and establishing herself within the community.

We had pretty much divided ourselves into two main groups as our team walked along ridges in an isolated part of the Annapurna Himalaya range. We were on a four-day trek along the ridges to the remote village of Siklis, an extremely isolated and representative of the Gurung ethnic culture.

I (Jeffrey) was walking in the A Group, about a half dozen fast-walkers who were well-conditioned and somewhat athletically inclined. The B Group was composed of the "strollers," those who liked to take their time, who were not in the best shape, or just preferred to lag behind and sing songs with the others.

If the A Group consisted of the serious trekkers, then the B Group were the social walkers—they liked to talk as they moved along, taking breaks at the bottom of each hilltop to rest, and more breaks at the top of each climb to recover. Kristine would move between each of our groups, but much of the time she preferred to walk alone.

The A Group stopped for lunch on the saddle between two hills, a clearing in the forest that allowed for gorgeous views of Macchapuchare (Fish Tail Mountain) and the Annapurna Massif. As we prepared to continue onward during the long day's walk, Kristine arrived at the spot for her own rest. We chatted for a few minutes and then began the next climb through the forest.

Several hours later, we arrived at camp and began helping the porters and Sherpas set up our tents and arrange our belongings to prepare for the cold winter night. We washed up a bit, changed clothes, and relaxed over hot tea, our sore feet propped up on chairs.

It wasn't until close to nightfall that the slower group limped into camp, sore, tired, and complaining about the challenging day. A few members could hardly talk and just went right to bed. The rest of us sat around the table to catch up on the day's events and it was during this conversation that we eventually noticed that Kristine wasn't there.

"We thought she was with you," I said in rising panic. "We saw her at lunch and assumed she waited for you guys before walking further."

The members of the B Group shook their heads, confessing that they hadn't seen her all day. They had assumed she was with us.

"Where could she have gone?" we all wondered. She had been walking between us. There was only one trail that followed the ridgeline. We hadn't passed a single settlement or village all day, nor even seen another person on the mountain.

But indeed, Kristine was gone. To add to our apprehension, we knew that Kristine had never been trekking before. She had no outdoor survival skills, nor even any experience. Her tentmate recalled that she was dressed only in a light parka and usually only carried one bottle of water. This was January, the dead of the winter, and we were deep in the mountains far from any civilization.

As night fell, with still no sign of Kristine, the two dozen porters and Sherpas launched a search party to look for her, retracing our steps. We built a huge bonfire as a beacon and settled in to wait for news of a rescue. We couldn't possibly imagine what had happened to her or where she had gone since there was only one trail. Had she fallen off a cliff? Had she injured herself? Theories abounded, but we were certain of one thing—there was no way she could survive the night.

By 10 P.M., most of the search party returned, shivering and exhausted, but with no news. They had set off in different directions, walking all the way back to the lunch spot, but found no sign of Kristine. They had called out her name over and over but heard nothing in return. To make matters worse, by this time it had started to snow—with lightning and thunder as an accompaniment. None of us had ever heard of a thunderstorm that included snow and ice. There was simply no way Kristine would be able to survive in this weather. We pictured her huddled beneath a tree, shivering uncontrollably, terrified and alone in the dark.

At this point, our team began to fall apart. We started arguing about whose fault this was, blaming our guides for not keeping a closer eye, blaming ourselves for not taking better care of Kristine, and finally settling on the idea that this was her fault for being such a loner. Why couldn't she stay with the group? As the night wore on, the anger turned into grief, many of us crying for her loss. More than anyone else, I felt responsible for her death. I would have to be the one to tell her parents and her friends that we had lost her.

Our guide was so despondent that he sent out other search parties throughout the night, continuing to offer optimistic encouragement that she had to be on the mountain somewhere; she couldn't possibly vanish into thin air. What was left unsaid is that indeed she could have easily "vanished into thin air" if she had fallen off a steep ridge.

We tried to sleep that night, but the raging storm, ground-shuddering thunder, freezing temperatures, and terrible grief kept most of us awake. Hopes, wishes, prayers, or luck led us to anticipate that the morning might bring us welcome news.

At first light I stuck my head out the tent flap to find several inches of snow blanketing the ground, as well as the mountain peaks surrounding us. Yet the search parties had retired, exhausted, with no evidence of Kristine anywhere. We had no choice but to continue onward toward Siklis, where we could at least find some way to call in a rescue team to locate her body.

We walked all that day grief-stricken and despondent, hardly noticing the spectacular scenery around us. Our conversations remained focused on theories of what could have possibly happened to Kristine, but none of them made much sense. We were just grasping at straws, trying to preserve some semblance of hope in the face of despair.

I'll let Kristine tell you the rest of the story from her perspective (so you now know that we did eventually become reunited).

KRISTINE: BEING TOO INDEPENDENT

I hadn't seen anyone all day since lunch, but that wasn't all that unusual since I was used to walking on my own, enjoying the time to think about things and move at my own pace. The long day was drawing to a close and I was surprised that I hadn't yet reached camp or seen anyone else in our group. It hadn't occurred to me that I might be lost because I thought I had stuck to the only trail.

Since dusk was fast approaching, I decided to stay put and call out for someone to find me, instead of possibly making my situation worse by moving around anymore in this region of steep hills and unfamiliar terrain. "Hello! Hello!" I called out every thirty seconds or so. Before long, two young men came into sight from the upper sections of the terraced fields around me. At first, I thought one of them was the guide who had handed me my box lunch earlier that day. Wasn't he wearing a red t-shirt like that? It didn't take long for me to realize that these men weren't our guides at all. In fact, they were Maoist guerrillas who were patrolling the area in the midst of a civil war that had already claimed tens of thousands of lives. How did I know they weren't part of our staff? For one thing, they were dressed differently than I had seen anyone before. And secondly, rather than smiling as they approached me, they had the look of stone killers. Oh, did I mention that they were carrying weapons?

For some reason, I did not feel fear at that moment. It was almost as if the guerrillas were as surprised to see me as I was to see them. Here I was, a lone light-haired, blue-eyed white woman, standing in the middle of the forest. Immediately, I put my hands together in front of me, slightly bowed my head and said, "Namaste." I was relieved to see them greet me the same way, the most natural response in a country where every man, woman, and child automatically says this, meaning, "I honor all the divine qualities in you."

Kristine after having been rescued by a Maoist patrol.

As the men climbed swiftly down the terraces, I approached them hoping they might assist me in some way. It never occurred to me at the time that they might take me prisoner, hold me for ransom, or harm me in some way. But, then, maybe I was desperate for anyone to show me the way out of the forest to reconnect with my friends. It didn't seem like I had any other choice except to trust them. If I ran from there, where would I go? So with few options, I put on my best smile and tried not to show any fear.

I remembered the name of the village where our group was eventually headed, so I repeated it, "Siklis, Siklis," and shrugged, using sign language to indicate I was lost.

The men nodded their understanding and pointed vaguely in a direction over a valley. I bowed my head and offered my thanks, then started slowly walking where they had indicated, having no clue how I would manage to get there on my own. To my relief, one of the men put his hands together by his ears, as if to suggest that sleeping quarters were not too far away. Still smiling from ear to ear, and mustering every expression of gratitude I had in me, I thanked them over and over again and set out toward the village below, called Chipli.

It wasn't too long before I came across a teenage boy who was herding water buffalo down the stone path that wound through the village. I was greeted by stares of curiosity, but more than that, by the warmth in the eyes of these strangers and the mutual greetings of "Namaste." As I approached the far end of the village, the view of the hillside and mountains in the distance was spectacular, but it didn't include any sign of my group anywhere.

I backtracked toward the schoolyard, where a lively volleyball game was underway. Perhaps the boys and men assembled there had seen other members of my group earlier in the day. One man came forward and asked me if he could help me—in English! It seemed that he had once worked for an oil company, so had learned the language on the job. Even more remarkable, he immediately invited me to stay with his family, since there were no lodges in this area, nor even any trekkers or tourists who ever ventured this far afield.

The village elders appeared to hold some kind of meeting to decide what to do with me. Regardless of the outcome of their discussion, my main concern was thinking about my group and how worried they must be about what happened to me. I supposed that would have to wait for another time, since my immediate priority was to find a place to sleep.

When I hesitated at the doorway of the man's house, his son encouraged me to enter, saying in English, "Come, come." So, looking as humble as I possibly could, I approached the hearth as the father explained the situation to the women gathered there. Through a combination of sign language, exaggerated facial expressions, and their basic English skills, they embraced me with a heartfelt concern for my well-being and safety. The young mother of two beckoned me to come closer, "Sister, sit down." "Sister, you drink?"

After initially being seated on a small, wicker stool, I soon joined the mother and the other young women gathered on a small carpet right next to the wood-burning fire. They would take turns feeding the fire, blowing on the embers through a bamboo tube, and boiling water for more tea. There was a storm brewing outside with swirling snow so I was very grateful for the shelter and the warmth of the fire. I felt more than a little guilty about the rest of my group who I knew were huddled in their tents worrying about me.

The family asked me a hundred questions. They wondered how old I was and where my husband and children were. They were dumbfounded when I told them I was 38 and had no husband or children. I could see their pity and discomfort with this unusual circumstance, considering that girls in their culture are married soon after puberty.

While the father was outside gathering firewood and the girls were at a neighbor's house watching television (their favorite American show was *Worldwide Wrestling*), the mother and I had a chance for "girl talk" as we sipped our tea. She asked me if girls and boys were treated the same in the United States, and I told her that my parents did not necessarily privilege my brother because he was male. She nodded in agreement with such practices, and then said "Nepalese culture no good" as she explained the difficult situation she was in, with only two daughters. Just then, her husband came in and assured me that it was okay, not to take what she was saying too seriously.

The father volunteered to guide me to Siklis the next day. During the walk, I saw the countryside in a way that had been inaccessible during the first couple of days of our trek. On this day, the father pointed out the various projects, such as bridges and water taps, which he told me were made possible by aid from countries like England. His explanations constantly reinforced the distinction he wanted to make clear to me, "Nepal's a poor country. No money. U.S. is rich. We need money." Back in Kathmandu the next week, I couldn't forget his disdain for the government authorities. At the same time, I was getting a better sense of the complexity of caste and ethnic hierarchies in Nepal, especially when a Brahmin friend of mine heard about my experiences in Chipli and readily characterized the Gurung people as "not very ambitious."

Jeffrey: Being Lost and Finding Your Way

We were still an hour away from our destination when the walkie-talkie I (Jeffrey) was carrying squawked, announcing a garbled message from our guide saying something about Kristine. I could barely make out what he was saying but understood enough that somehow they had located our lost member and that she was actually waiting for us at the camp. They had found her; or rather maybe she had found us.

The reunion was both emotional and dramatic, with lots of hugging and crying. We had believed our lost comrade was dead and now heard her amazing story of rescue by guerrillas and her subsequent "home-stay" in a village. While we were freezing and crying in our snow-blown tents, she had been nestled in a warm house by a fire.

I found the aftermath of this adventure the most interesting. Kristine was a strong, independent, resourceful woman, an accomplished professional, who was used to depending on herself. She lived alone and liked being alone. Yet now, a floodgate of emotion had opened when she saw how much we cared about her and how devastated we had been.

Without conscious intention, Kristine began talking about the ways she protected herself from hurt—and from intimacy. She confessed that she had a destructive relationship waiting for her when she returned home, and that she had no idea how to get this guy out of her apartment—he had decided to move in without her consent or approval. When a few of us volunteered to act as her advocates and support system, she was moved to share at an even deeper level some self-defeating patterns. The result from this trauma was that we had become an even more close-knit family.

People make resolutions all the time and swear that they will take certain actions that are good for them. In this case, with the support of a few of us in the group, Kristine did make a number of changes that had been needed for some time. And none of this would have been possible if she hadn't gotten lost in the first place.

KRISTINE: THE AFTERMATH

The biggest thing that I got out of this experience was the realization that no matter what I do or say, or how I am in the world, other people are going to react (or not) based more on their own personal background and the experiences that they've had in their life, than on anything that I did or said. I was concerned with how the other members of the group would react to my getting lost (e.g., their anger, sadness, etc.), but I ultimately realized that I have no control over that. I don't have to carry the burden of worrying about not getting them angry or not making them sad. I am constantly reminded of that realization in my life "post-Nepal" when I am in situations of conflict or tension. For example, if my department chair becomes angry, I used to feel like I had to ward off that anger, or be the "good, nice girl" who would defuse that tension, but now I am more aware that if he gets angry, that's his problem, not mine.

I started therapy soon after I returned from Nepal, and my therapist helped me realize how powerless I really am when it comes to controlling other people's emotions. She often pointed this out in a humorous way when I would tell her how convinced I was of my power to influence other people. She would make a joke about how "powerful" I am. I had such a good, trusting, open relationship with her that I could take that kind of joke and then laugh at myself (although there were times I was still convinced of my power!) and slowly start to recognize patterns in those situations of conflict and tension.

Perhaps the biggest immediate change in my life in Nepal was the sense of relief that I felt when I told some of the group members on the trip about my destructive relationship back home with a guy who was potentially dangerous. The "real" life-changing experience for me occurred once I was out in the woods. I was carrying around so much shame and fear related to this relationship, thinking the absolute worst would happen. I was obsessed with these skeletons in my closet, but once I began talking about the situation, things didn't seem so overwhelming. None of this could have happened if I hadn't felt so vulnerable and lost after the episode. None of the people with me tried to judge me; if anything they liked me more than before. This gave me the strength to talk to people I love back home, and I got the same supportive reactions. In many cases, revealing my vulnerability often helped others to tell me personal, painful stories from their past.

Ironically, this trip halfway around the world to Nepal influenced my commitment to social justice more on the local than the global level. Of course, I still focus on teaching Asian and world history, and I share with my students a sense of a commitment to global social justice through the readings I assign and the topics we discuss in class. But the whole process of being true to myself (it must sound like a cliché, but it's really true!) has made me more focused on my immediate surroundings and more eager to fulfill my potential as a strong, committed member of the local community. For example, after thinking about the issue of sexual slavery in Nepal, I've done more reading on that topic and have shared articles and books with my students on this global phenomenon, but I have also become involved with the local taskforce against human trafficking and have tried to raise awareness about this issue as a local phenomenon.

Living a Dream—That is Now Ending

I'm a football player in a big-time program. It's taken me a long time to get to where I am, and now I'm living the dream. I love football. It's what I was put here on this planet to do. On a game-day morning, I just get so pumped, it's like no other feeling in the world. I know that I only have one year of this left, since I'm graduating next spring. I've been one of the better players in our league, but coach says I don't have the size to play in the pros. I've focused so much of my life on football that I don't really know what else to do now. A few years ago another player was in this same situation, and he went into the Peace Corps. He said it was the best thing he ever did. It seems like such a different world from the football world, but maybe that's what I need.

BEING LOST IN OTHER WAYS

It is perhaps not surprising that an experience like Kristine's changed her life forever, or at least altered her trajectory significantly. In the most difficult times, when your resources and resolve are tested, eliciting strong emotional reactions, you are most likely to experience the deepest and most lasting impact of your helping efforts. The lesson learned, whether you are working abroad or in your own community, is that when you encounter challenges that you feel are beyond your capability, when you feel overwhelmed and ill-equipped, when you are lost and can't find your way—*that* is when you have the best opportunity to stretch yourself in new ways. These may not be situations that you would deliberately choose (who enjoys being lost?), but they are the situations that can have the most impact.

Although the preceding example refers to being physically lost, a similar sensation is associated with feeling rudderless in the direction your life is taking. College is a time of exploration, of trial and error, of new experiences that are designed to help you to find a place for yourself in which you can feel productive. Yet this journey is often confusing and frustrating, especially when you consider how often the average person changes his or her mind about possible career paths.

Struggling for a Purpose

Well, it's been three years since I've graduated from college, and things aren't exactly working out like I thought they would. I'm working in a job [real estate] I can't stand, which is fine but I at least thought I would be making more money than I am. I've always been a money guy. I totally like nice things, and I don't know how I could survive without them! I drive a BMW, but I can't really afford it. My bosses really encourage us to drive nice cars and wear fancy clothes, because it will help us create a certain image and attract new business. If I stick at this for another 10 years, I feel confident that I'll be successful and making good money, but right now I can't stand it. I feel like I'm at a point where I need to commit to another 10 years on the job or leave and begin something new. One of the problems with this job is that I don't really feel like I have a purpose in the world. The only person I'm really trying to help by doing this is myself, and if I'm miserable, why am I even doing it?

Unless you choose to work within your own community, the place in which you have spent most of your life, the environment in which you are familiar with every nuance and bump in the road, service work involves considerable adaptation and flexibility. Particularly when you work in foreign lands, your knowledge of local customs and language is likely to be inadequate and flawed. As much as you want to be helpful, you will likely commit multiple mistakes and misjudgments based on your ignorance and lack of experience within that world. The good news is that if you demonstrate sufficient modesty, humility, sensitivity, and respect, local people will give you the benefit of the doubt, and perhaps even find your foibles endearing if not amusing. When I (Jeffrey) was teaching in Peru for a period of time, one of my colleagues there kept a special notebook in which he jotted down all the humorous ways that I mangled Spanish through my creative attempts to invent words that seemed perfectly suitable to me.

I should know better, yet I am continuously surprised by the innumerable ways that I am caught off-guard by what appears to be going on around me. The truth of the matter is that most of the time that I'm working abroad, I don't have a clear idea at all about what is happening, nor what it means. My mastery of the Nepali language is limited to ordering tea the way I like it (black, no sugar, with just a little milk), asking permission to take a photograph, and talking to children about their names, ages, and how they like school. I often find myself in strange situations in which all I can do is grin stupidly and try my best not to be too judgmental about what seems so chaotic and confusing around me.

Back home, I become more than a little annoyed when people answer their cell phones while we are in the middle of a conversation or talk in loud voices while in public settings, as if they are either alone or don't really care who they are disturbing. But in meetings that take place in Nepal, even in high-level negotiations, we are constantly interrupted by individuals who insist on answering their phones no matter what is going on—and then proceed to carry on lengthy conversations while everyone else in the room waits. During one conference in which I was speaking on stage to a large group of health professionals, I counted no less than seven officials who were talking on their phones in loud voices while I was trying to concentrate on my speech. It was almost as if they were conducting the conversations as much for public consumption as to carry on any business with the caller. Maybe that was the point and it has eluded me.

The students who are with me have their sensibilities challenged when they learn that such phone behavior is not only common throughout the country but also a sign of status and power. But their worlds are turned upside down in so many other ways. They learn that malnutrition and tuberculosis are the leading causes of death around these parts; for women, childbirth presents the greatest danger, especially because obstetric care is so rare (except for Kiran). The students who join me on our expeditions carry on conversations with local students and discover that adolescent girls, during their first menstruation, are put in isolation for one to three weeks in a darkened room. They are not permitted to encounter water, light, or a male face. Every Nepalese girl in the room confessed to this treatment, admitting that it is both crazy and archaic, yet they also agreed that they might very well carry on this tradition with their own daughters.

One of the turning points that may occur when immersing yourself in another culture is actually joining with local people in their rituals and experiencing them from the inside. This type of experience allows you to develop greater understanding and sensitivity to their life and challenges, as well as break down cultural barriers.

Many of the discussions that take place among the students who are working abroad are centered around the strange customs they notice, increasing their awareness of behavior they take for granted. Several of the women were heard laughing about the worst all-time pick-up approach they'd yet encountered when a man approached them and said, "You wanna see something really cool?"

Of course they immediately agreed, excited that they had met one of the local guys. The man then proceeded to show them a video he had captured on his cell phone that showed a goat being sacrificed, blood spraying everywhere, the head falling to the ground after a hard whack with a machete. This was only one of so many ways their views of reality were challenged. For instance, drivers in Nepal honk their horns not in anger, never in anger, but as a courtesy to others to let them know they are passing. Drivers also use their turn signals not to cue an upcoming turn or lane change (there are no organized lanes) but to indicate to those behind that it is (reasonably) safe to pass. It was particularly confusing to the students that Nepalese people almost never say no to any question or request, even if they have no intention of ever following through; it is just considered impolite to say no to a visitor. Even more baffling is that the Nepalese shake their head from side to side to say yes, rather than no. And the students crossed signals repeatedly when they waved their hands to people by wiggling their fingers (which means "come here") instead of moving the hand side to side.

Before we express amazement, we have to consider what visitors from this part of the world would think of our customs. I mentioned previously about when a Nepalese student first arrived at our university, she could only shake her head in amusement upon learning that people in our country actually keep their animals indoors and that we spend valuable resources to feed dogs and cats and parakeets that provide no future nourishment for us. She watched owners walk their dogs, picking up the animal's poop and carefully putting it in a bag. As if this wasn't disgusting enough, she was also shocked to learn our filthy custom of wearing shoes inside the house. For such a supposedly civilized country, she found us very "primitive" in some of our customs.

Dilemmas occur all the time, making it difficult to sort out what is genuine, what is a misperception, and what is a gross misunderstanding or miscalculation. In the poorer nations of the world, where people have so little, individuals are often playing some angle to take advantage of situations. Corruption is rampant. Everyone wants a piece of the pie, their allocated share of any money or resources, plus another large piece for their own friends and families. Those with a soft heart and little understanding for the underlying dynamics can not only become an easy mark but actually reinforce dysfunctional patterns.

Once set loose in the urban, chaotic sprawl of Kathmandu, team members often wander around shopping and exploring the city. A mother approaches you with an adorable baby in her arms. You start to turn away, expecting someone else who wants to sell you something—*pashmina* scarves, counterfeit goods, or hashish. But instead the woman says simply that she and her baby haven't eaten in two days. Would it be possible for you to purchase the baby some milk?

You are caught off guard. She isn't asking for money, just milk for her starving baby. How could you—or anyone else—possibly refuse? So of course you agree and since you spy a market nearby, you ask her to follow you inside. You fill a basket with milk, but also a few other basic staples of flour, vegetables, and rice. The woman's face tells you that you may have quite literally saved her life with your generosity. You leave the store with a huge grin on your face, escorting the mother and baby with their bag of precious food, then carry on your way. Never have you felt so good about doing a good deed that cost so little and yet made such a huge difference in someone's life.

But if you stopped and looked back over your shoulder, you might very well see the woman head back into the shop, where she actually works as an employee. Her "job" is to reel in unsuspecting tourists and get them to buy her food, which she then returns to the store, where the owner gives her a few rupees for her trouble. The money is used to purchase drugs.

Thickening Our Skins

So far, many of the stories we have told are about the amazing privilege it is to help people most in need. We have shared success stories (with more to follow) about the impact that almost anyone with good intentions can have. Yet we live in a world of deception, greed and, yes, desperation. Those of us who try to enter the communities of the less fortunate must also be prepared to thicken our skins and navigate through very confusing situations—some we can barely understand.

In some of the villages where we work, powerful men have threatened to sabotage our efforts if we don't provide them with some benefit for their own kin. It may seem as if we have overly romanticized the altruistic efforts, but we have also tried to portray honestly the hardships you would face—physical, psychological, and spiritual.

We mention these examples not to be cynical or discouraging, but rather to emphasize all the ways that you will feel lost when working within strange cultures. And let's face it: *anywhere* you start a new job is going to be a "foreign culture" to you in which you don't speak the local "dialect" nor understand the organizational rituals and customs. Feeling lost is not only inevitable; it is to be expected. The question, then, is not what you will do *if* you should find yourself in way over your head in any new assignment, but rather how you will handle the predictable confusion, disorientation, and challenges, no matter how well prepared you might believe yourself to be.

CHAPTER 7

Student Transformations

What is the enduring impact of a helping journey, even if it lasts just a few weeks? One of the major themes of this book is how devoting time to serve others can also have a tremendous influence on the course of your own life.

There are so many classes you take, workshops you attend, conversations you have, in which you make sincere declarations that things will change. You resolve to do things differently, to apply what you learned. You make promises that you never keep. You forget what it was that seemed so important. You sell your books. You throw away your notes. Memories fade with time. Supposed transformations become temporary. You move on to the next thing. You regress, slip back, or jump into familiar, old patterns.

There are, of course, limits to what you can learn in a classroom, in books, on videos, or from the Internet. Even when these experiences are interactive, they are also relatively passive; you are sitting still and receiving, a receptacle being filled up with stuff. There is only so much you can take in and hold, especially when you are inundated with media, speeches, e-mail, phone calls, text messages, video games, lectures, discussions, conversations, readings, films, all of which are endlessly bombarding you.

That is why field studies and service learning are such a critical part of learning a profession or mastering a set of skills. You experiment with strategies or concepts in the real world. You observe people and situations as they are, instead of as you were told they would be. You become actively engaged with people, emotionally aroused in ways that can't happen sitting still. You *live* what you have learned. Classroom and book learning provide a foundation of knowledge, but then you must invest the hard work to make the content part of you. That is why most professional training includes some component of service learning, field studies, practica, and internships. You are asked to apply and use what you have learned.

RETURN FROM THE JOURNEYS

One of the most challenging aspects of any transformative experience is to hold on to the momentum once it is over. You complete a class or return from a trip, and what happens next? All too often, the honest answer is that you move on to something else that takes priority.

Among those who went to Nepal, there was a period of readjustment and re-entry once they returned home. One person on the trip quit his job the day he returned, deciding that he was tired of the petty politics within his institution, especially compared to what he could be doing with his time to make more of a difference without such restraints. Another person announced to her husband that she wanted a divorce after experiencing the intense intimacy of the group support and comparing it to the relatively superficial communication she had grown accustomed to at home. Even though I (Jeffrey) have been to Nepal a half-dozen times, and also have seen a dozen similar environments, I decided to step down from my administrative responsibilities after returning to work (as I am writing these words). I realized that it's time to stop dabbling; I have to free up time to devote more of myself to this work. But it's more than that: after being in such a different place, I realized that I'm simply tired of doing the same things year after year. I felt inspired to reinvent myself once again, a makeover that I've initiated once every few years to keep myself excited about what I'm doing.

In this chapter, we tell the stories of several students who went to Nepal and talk about their personal transformations, as well as their fears that the effects would not endure. You may find yourself identifying with some of the struggles retold in these case examples and resonating with their experiences.

JANE: "I SAW A PHOTO ON THE WALL"

Once upon a time, human beings were channeled into professions (rarely did they ever have a choice) that were expected to last for the whole of their (brief) lifetimes. Eldest sons inherited their father's land, middle sons became soldiers, and youngest sons became priests (women were married off). Eons before that, everyone was a hunter or a gatherer, a farmer or a baby-maker. In more modern times (the last 1,000 years or so), the options expanded to tool-maker, blacksmith, stone mason, merchant—or whatever craft you inherited from your parents.

Only during relatively recent times could you actually make your own choices regarding a future—attend a university, pick a profession such as teacher, engineer, artist, entrepreneur, plumber, scientist, or whatever—and pursue this until retirement or death. It is all the more remarkable that nowadays, the average person might follow several distinctly different career paths during a lifespan that is now triple what it was several thousand years ago. Whatever job you think you are preparing for today may bear little resemblance to what you end up doing each subsequent decade thereafter. Not only does the average college student change majors three or more times prior to graduation, but professionals may very well work just as many lines of employment.

Every decade or so since graduation, I (Jeffrey) have worked in very different professions I could never have imagined. I originally started out in business and sales, then became a preschool teacher and then a school counselor, believing I was a finished product. I went back to school to become a psychologist and then a professor, certain in my 20s that my path was finally set. Yet most recently, I have been working primarily as an administrator and writer, and I can already see my next career developing on the horizon—running a charitable foundation. I wouldn't be surprised at all if my path takes a few more twists and turns before retirement.

Keeping in mind the various stages of career development that evolve as we age and mature, a grandmother approaching 60, Jane Kinsley, decided to go back to school to create a new life after a divorce and several medical problems forced her to make new adaptations.

Jane began a graduate program in counseling, found enjoyment in this new field, and studied earnestly to redefine herself once again, to find a new purpose and mission for her life. Although I did not know Jane, she was walking by my office one day when she spied a photo attached to the bulletin board on the wall. It was a picture I had taken six years earlier (during my second visit

The photo that inspired Jane to get involved in the project helping neglected girls stay in school. The four girls on the left are still in school; The girl on the right "disappeared."

to Nepal) of five girls playing together in the village square. They were girls from lower-caste families, destined for early marriage at puberty or, if unlucky, perhaps given to "job brokers" who might sell them to brothels in India.

When Jane saw the photo, she had an instantaneous, visceral reaction that struck something deep within her. "For some reason," she recalled, "tears came to my eyes when I saw the girls' sweet, shy smiles and twinkly eyes. I felt an instant love, almost a bond with these girls from Nepal."

Jane stopped to read the newspaper article that accompanied the photo and learned about the poverty and deprivation in these villages, the civil war going on at the time, and the high likelihood that so many of these girls would end up sold into slavery. She decided in that moment, impulsively yet with finality, that she would visit these girls. She must go to Nepal to see this for herself and do something to help them. If she had been questioned at that moment, Jane would have been hard-pressed to explain this decision or how it came to be. In many ways, it made no sense whatsoever, since she was in the middle of her graduate program, had health problems, was struggling financially, and had a number of family obligations.

"Every night for months, I would see the children's faces and wonder what they were doing and how they were surviving. What were they like? How did they spend their time? I just couldn't get them out of my mind. I was so taken by their innocent little faces that I composed a letter to all my friends and family asking them to help me provide scholarships."

Jane managed to raise more than $6,000 in the coming months, enough not only to sustain these five girls all the way through college, but several others as well. She also decided to join the next team for a visit and make it her mission to track down the five girls. While the rest of the group went on a weeklong trek as a reward for their efforts, Jane remained behind in the village to work in the schools. She lived near the main square, sipped tea with local parents, and taught English in both the elementary and high school.

One of the first mornings that Jane entered the classroom, she was greeted by the children singing her a welcome song. As she prepared for her lesson, scanning the rows of more than fifty children squeezed into the dark room, her eyes fell on one shy-looking girl who appeared familiar. It was her! It was one of the girls from the photograph, now six years older but with that same twinkle in her eye. Jane pulled out the photograph that she kept with her always and compared the faces.

"My eyes filled with tears. After eight months, I had found one of the children, the first of four that I was able to locate. Unfortunately the fifth girl, the one on the far right, disappeared somewhere. No one knows what happened to her, whether she was sold or her family just moved away. This first girl in my classroom was a bit nervous from all my attention, and she looked to a friend for reassurance. But then when I showed her the photo, and explained in simple English that I had been trying to find her she seemed to understand. She hugged me and it was a moment I will never forget."

Jane has since returned to the village, spending a longer period of time with the friends she has made. She found that once she returned home, her experiences with the children seemed like a dream; she had to go back, this time better prepared for what she would encounter and better equipped to offer more effective assistance.

Jane is already making plans to return again some time in the future, unwilling to let this project go and move on with the rest of her life. She has been struggling to find a new job that provides the kind of satisfaction and exhilaration that she experienced teaching in the village schools. At age 60, in many ways she sees her life is just beginning.

HEATHER: "SHARING A COMMON SPIRIT OF FEARLESS DREAMING"

Heather is a third-grade teacher, a graduate student, and also a mother of three children. Yet with all her commitments, which involve juggling her responsibilities in her job, at home, and at school, she has been hungry to make some changes in her life. Heather is the kind of teacher you always wish you had in elementary school—patient, loving, and supportive, but also highly skilled at motivating kids to reach beyond what they think they can do.

Even with all the stress going on in her life, Heather negotiated with her principal, instructors, and family to take the time (and spend the money) to go to Nepal—in the middle of the semester! She was also struggling with physical problems that prevented her from walking without excruciating pain, as well as some personal problems that occupied her mind. In other words, she had a lot of reasons and excuses not to do something like travel halfway around the world. Yet she decided that this was something she was going to do, no matter what obstacles stood in her way—financial, physical, school-related, job-related, or related to her family.

When faced with opportunities to take constructive risks, go off on adventures, or do something completely new, it is common to hear people supply a host of reasons why they can't follow through. They are even "good" excuses, meaning that they are totally legitimate reasons why such a move would not be very convenient or well timed. There are finances to consider, responsibilities and commitments, family obligations, health concerns, and so on. Yet it is also interesting how, once you decide to do something that is really, really important to you, you can somehow find a way to make it happen. That is the way that Heather thought about the challenge of putting her trip together in spite of opposition and resistance, both within herself and from others.

Heather jumped into this experience with all the enthusiasm and dedication she brings to everything she did. She raised extraordinary sums of money from friends and family to support the project. She got her third-grade class involved as well, educating the children about where she was going and what she was going to be doing. Most of the children were from immigrant families themselves, and participated in discussions about ways that everyone could make the world a better place and help those who are most needy. They donated their quarters and dollars to help the children in Nepal. The children wrote letters to Jeffrey about their reactions to their teacher leaving for such an exotic locale that was far beyond their understanding. Here is one representative letter:

Dear Dr. Kottler,

I hope you are a nice teacher. Our teacher is nervous about going to Nepal. Are you nervous when you go there? I feel sad that the children are poor because they can't go to school. If I was in Nepal and I was rich I'd will still give people money.

Your friend,
Athela

Like any good teacher, it was important for Heather to model for her students the qualities that she most wanted them to develop, which in this case was a sense of altruism and caring for others. Heather spends much of her life taking care of others—her students, her children, her friends, anyone who has a need. So this trip represented a huge step for her to start taking better care of herself.

As is so often the case with any important adventure, the journey begins with the preparation and contemplation long before the trip actually begins.

HEATHER'S STORY—IN HER OWN WORDS

Once I accepted the invitation to Nepal I noticed my process beginning. I began preparing myself physically, mentally, and spiritually for the trip. I knew it would be physically challenging because of Nepal's terrain and then there was that seven-day trek through the Himalayan Mountains, so I began working out with extra strength to prepare myself for what lay ahead. Mentally I began to gather as much information as I could about Nepal. Somehow, gathering information helped me to at least understand basic facts and customs that I might encounter on my developing adventure. Spiritually, I felt incredible peace at the core mission. I knew it was the right thing to do, and I felt this was going to be a tremendous blessing in my life. It was an honor to work for these girls and to be a part of something that was much bigger than me. Little did I know the true blessings that would be mine.

I was not prepared for the variety of reactions and support I received from friends and family. The support I received from most friends was tremendous, and they responded generously to my donation requests, which helped to raise enough money for many years of education. It was not the money they gave, but the hopeful spirit and the intention behind their giving that really was the gift. I was amazed by most individuals' feelings of inspiration and hope for these girls, which I felt was indirectly a hope and inspiration for what is good in life. I realized this mission was not only about the girls and helping them. This mission was way bigger than that; by being a part of this project, each person who learned about it and felt compassion and well wishes toward our friends in Nepal was blessed by the very feelings he or she had for them. They were blessed through the mission as well. Their hearts were touched with love and caring, and this is truly a blessing. There were a few, shocking to me, who did not support or engage on this level of listening and caring, and I felt so sad about their poorness in spirit. I felt such compassion for some of my family and friends, because I could see that their own feelings of deprivation kept them from reaching out to others, and this lack of hope was greatly saddening to me.

When we finally arrived in Kathmandu, the capital city of Nepal, I felt a stirring of interest and amusement at the organic collaged layout of the place. I found myself thinking, "What in the heck were they thinking when they made that city?" As I looked at the buildings and homes below, I saw they were spread all about without seeming to have any kind of order. I was not used to seeing a city built with what appeared to me to be chaotic disorganization. I knew then that I was in a different world and that this would be a special adventure. It has been said that "we see what we know, making it hard for us to see what others see." With this in mind, I knew that I must set aside my Western judgments and open my eyes, my mind, and my heart to try and fully understand what it was that I was about to experience. I feel fortunate to be a person who is open to different ways of being, and I am fascinated by how others view the world, so you can imagine my exhilaration at the potential learning experiences that were ahead of me. Embracing Nepal meant releasing my expectations. This offered me more than I could have imagined: it offered me the path to true happiness within myself.

My constant partner throughout the trip was Jane, whose story you read earlier. Jane modeled strength, courage, grace, compassion, dedication and humor the entire time we were together. She and I laughed so hard during the entire trip, and honestly, I have never had such fun in all my life! Jane and I climbed to Buddhist sacred sites; navigated crossing dirt roads while dodging rickshaws, water buffalo, motorcycles, overloaded buses, and bicycles; walked through thousands of festivalgoers who wanted to take our pictures; rode elephants on safari, canoed down sacred rivers with crocodiles; and survived stomach upsets and interesting unknown menu items. We became enthusiastic connoisseurs of Nepalese milk tea. Jane helped me process not only my daily culture shocks and experiences, but also many personal issues that I had been struggling with the past two years since beginning the counseling program. She also killed a very large hairy spider in our room that overlooked the Himalayan mountain range. My hero!

I learned that the teachers in Nepal are fearless dreamers. Despite all our differences, we understand a common spirit language of hope and love through teaching. The teachers I met in Nepal are like teachers in America; we believe in the impossible and we sleep a little, and dream a lot! As I looked into their eyes, I saw their dreams for their students, dreams that are the same as ours: to provide quality education to students, to give them the best future possible, and to help them reach their full potential and grow to be happy healthy productive citizens in the world. What a privilege it is to help those who help themselves.

I am inspired and empowered by these brave men, women, and children that I met. I am motivated beyond words to help these noble souls reach their goals of providing quality education to their students. We are so privileged here in America, and we have such excesses in material items, I think we can share a little to help others to reach their dreams.

Each person I met reaffirmed my belief in the strength and inherent goodness in humans. I had the privilege of teaching in a variety of classrooms while visiting the schools. As I stood in the front of the classroom, I could feel the teacher watching me, reading me, and I knew that inside we were the same. They understood this as well, and strong bonds developed between us in a short time. As I taught these beautiful Nepalese children, I felt transformed and renewed, just as I feel when I teach in America. I felt like we are all connected — I have always

Heather stands proudly with the Nepalese children she taught.

believed that, but that day teaching in Bandipur Class Five, *I got it*! I understood on a complete physical, emotional, and intellectual level; it was huge!

When first I arrived in Nepal I felt sorry for the poor students and people I met, and I felt that I had a lot to offer them, but through continued interaction with these gentle, loving, kind, funny, resourceful, intelligent, spiritually rich, and astoundingly delightful people, I began to realize how rich *they* were and how much I gained from them as a result of our meeting. How can it be? I came to give and help here, and I did give and help. But now I was leaving richer than when I came. Amazing!

What was it? What made such a difference in my life? Was it the work and training as part of my program at the university? Was it being thrust into a new and challenging environment and being open to change? Was it being a part of a meaningful humanitarian project that makes a real difference in the lives of many? Maybe it was experiencing a culture that actually cares for their collective group, and seeing those secure attachments? Was it having caring individuals who would help me process my experiences whenever I pleased? Could it possibly be the sacred moments on the trip, such as praying on top of the Buddhist camp site or communing with God on the Rapti River? What helped me transcend and integrate my experiences and brought me to a deeper understanding and ability within myself? Today I feel empowered, energized, balanced, and *happy*! I came home with strength and a commitment to live a more authentic life and I am.

Although I am not exactly sure what caused it, I know I changed as a result of my experiences in Nepal, and I feel extremely blessed and thankful for the entire process. I look forward to a long and prosperous relationship with my friends in Nepal. We share a common spirit, and we still have so much to learn from each other.

Like Jane, Heather found that one trip to the villages was only a tease, just enough to capture her passion but also leave her wanting much more. Heather was so utterly transformed by the experience that, upon returning, she turned her whole life upside down, reorienting her priorities. She immediately made plans to return to Nepal twice more the following year. She redoubled her efforts to raise money for the children's education. She wrote a grant to support technological improvements in schools there. And she undertook a research project to investigate ways that other students and professionals have been dramatically impacted by working in other cultures. Her children, her colleagues, her fellow students, and her friends would all attest that Heather is no longer the same person they previously knew.

CHRISTINE: "I FOUND A SECOND HOME"

Christine describes herself as "risk-avoidant." She had never traveled to another culture and was somewhat timid about trying new things, much less challenging herself to go way outside her usual boundaries. Throughout her life, she has struggled with fears and anxieties.

"I was one of those people who grew up with a lot of fear. Anything that pushed me outside the little box of my reality caused me anxiety. This manifested itself in frustration, shame, embarrassment, or usually all three. Fortunately, I became a dancer at a very young age, and passionately studied ballet through college. There is a certain level of commitment to dance at that level. For me, that commitment did not leave much time for anything else, which meant that, like an ostrich, I could bury my head in the ballet world, and not have to push myself outside of my box very often."

Christine remembers when she decided to give up dancing professionally after a lifetime of total commitment to her art. In letting go of this identity, she was surprised by how much freedom she had to reinvent herself in new ways. She realized that for the first time in her life, she had space to try new options, experiment with alternative ways of being, even take risks that she would have never considered previously because of the way she had defined herself. The fears and apprehensions were still there, but for the first time she felt excited about moving ahead anyway, despite the trepidation.

Before she knew it, Christine was on a bus in Kathmandu, driving through a scene that seemed out of a circus—cows sleeping in the middle of the road, rickshaws, tractors, scooters, minibuses, trucks, bicycles, pedestrians, and water buffalo all sharing the traffic. It was all so overwhelming that Christine seemed to shut down; she just couldn't make sense of everything she was experiencing and observing. She could feel herself regressing, like the fearful child she had once been—and then felt tremendous shame that she wasn't more in control.

"It was our first full day in Kathmandu," Christine remembers, "and we were getting ready to go out for sightseeing. Our first stop was a Buddhist temple, then on to a medieval village. Without thinking, I put on jeans and a tank top, and tied a sweater around my waist. When I got down to the hotel lobby to meet everyone, a fellow traveler pulled me aside for a minute. She said she just wanted to let me know that baring my shoulders in the temple might be offensive to some of the Nepalese people, so I might want to put something on over my tank top. I immediately got upset, not with her for bringing it to my attention, but with myself. I was so embarrassed for my mistake, and so angry with myself for not even thinking about cultural sensitivity. Even though I wasn't the only one in that position that day, I felt really stupid."

As the days and weeks continued, Christine slowly began to gain confidence and start to feel, if not comfortable, then at least accustomed to the strange things she was constantly encountering. Yet once she began to get a handle on the emotional strains, the physical demands of the trek through the mountains threw her for another loop. Even though she was a well-conditioned dancer, Christine really struggled the first few days with climbing the endless steps that weave up and down through the rice-terraced peaks and valleys. At one point, she was ready to give up—and probably would have, if she could have figured out a way to get back down! She had no choice but to continue the slog up over the next ridge.

Although the trekking was at times very challenging, Christine was most moved by her contact with the girls in the villages.

"I am still searching for a way to accurately describe what it was like to watch the young girls receive their scholarships. When it was my turn to give away one of the scholarships, I cried. The little girl was so proud, yet so overcome with all of the attention. She kept hiding her face in her hands, then smiling, then looking away from me. I felt such a connection to her at that moment that it brought me to tears; she seemed overwhelmed with the ceremony, and in that space I think I knew how she felt.

"At that time, I was still adjusting to everything about the country: the people, the language, the food, the time change . . . everything. I was on complete sensory overload at that point. That little girl's reaction snapped me out of some serious culture shock. I could immediately relate to how she acted and felt. In such a foreign place, her reaction was so familiar that it just grounded me. For the first time in my life, I really got a sense of the universality of feelings and emotions."

Another part of the trip that had a huge impact on Christine was a visit to a local college, where she spent much of the day talking with students. During one session with nursing students, she had the opportunity to get into some very personal and intimate conversations, comparing their lives. She was amazed by the courage of these young women who defied their families' expectations that they get married in order to pursue a career.

"During this time, I got the opportunity to share with them a little about what I'm studying at school. This was really an honor for me to be a teacher for others. Other people in our group asked the women questions about sexuality in Nepal. It was amazing how open and honest the girls were in their answers. We talked about the tradition of isolating a girl when she menstruates. Most

Christine pictured with some of the children in the village.

girls in the room went through that. When I asked them if they would continue that custom with their daughters, the majority said a very adamant 'no!' It was a growing experience for me to see that even though that ritual is part of their culture, some of the women were determined to change the tradition. Again, it taught me about the universality of feelings and emotions. Just because their culture and customs are so different from mine does not mean that we as women are so far apart."

There was so little time for Christine to make sense of what she was hearing and seeing and living. With her head reeling and her heart aching, she would be rushed off to the van for another visit to a village or meeting. There was little, if any, downtime or periods for reflection. It was one adventure after another, almost to the point that she had no room to take in anything else new.

"I had so many ups and downs during this trip, many joys and many frustrations. A lot of the time, I felt like I was at the bottom of the learning curve, and this was extremely frustrating. I struggled a lot, especially during the trek, but I never quit. I never gave up. Though both the laughter and the tears, I knew I was on a journey that would change me forever. The lessons I learned in Nepal about myself, about other people, and about other worlds would shape me for the rest of my life."

Once she returned, people asked her what was different. What did she learn about herself? How was she changed? These are questions that she still struggles to understand.

"It's not that I don't have answers; I just can't quite find the words to describe them. I was hoping to learn not to sweat the small stuff, and to define what was really 'important' in life. That didn't happen. I still get frustrated when I'm stressed, upset when I fail, and hurt when I'm rejected. Those are basic human emotions that I will always feel. Even though I can't put words to it, I know that what changed in me is bigger than just emotions or feelings. It is an understanding of how big the world is, but how closely we are connected. I never had an opportunity to learn that lesson before. But that is only a part of what changed for me. A bigger part is the difference I can feel in my heart, a difference I feel both literally and figuratively. That is what I can't find words for.

"There is a part of my heart that will stay in Nepal forever. Now that I am home, I find that to be so true. Nepal feels familiar now. When I think back to the first few days and how shocking it all was to me, I almost can't relate to those memories. I know the next time I go back, it will be like visiting an old friend."

ALI: "WHO REALLY LIVES IN POVERTY?"

Like Christine, Ali was a dancer until she found herself burned out with the rigorous demands of her profession. With just a year left before graduation, she switched majors to psychology and began investigating what she might do with her life off the stage. When an article appeared in the school paper about the project in Nepal, Ali made a call immediately to see how she could get on board. With tremendous passion and excitement, she raised a small fortune for the project, mostly small donations from fellow students and friends.

"The idea of going on this mission was based on everything I believe in most passionately," Ali explained, "helping others, providing hope for a better life, feeling a sense of accomplishment. The only problem was that we were going to a place where I felt very frightened and threatened. Everything would be different—the food, habits, religion, customs, everything. I just didn't think I could handle this very well. It all seemed so primitive."

Indeed, Ali did struggle those first few days, adjusting to the new sights and sounds, unfamiliar customs, and chaotic stimuli. She had prepared as well as she could for this trip, raising substantial sums of money from friends and family to support the children. Yet she was also hesitant and lacked confidence in her abilities. One turning point occurred at the end of the first week, when she visited with a group of nursing students. After some negotiation, she managed to get the instructor to leave the room so that she might have some private time with these young women her own age.

"They were all so genuinely curious about everything," Ali remembered. "The questions they had for us were intelligent and fun to answer. It was an amazing feeling, knowing that words that came out of my mouth directly contributed to their learning experience. For once, I was the teacher. I felt honored to answer them, especially when I felt like I really knew what I was talking about. It was amazing to witness their eyes being opened as I spoke. The same went for all of us whenever we asked them a question. I felt honored to learn about their culture from their point of view, because they are the ones living it. During this conversation, I felt very connected to these students. I realized that this was, in my opinion, the best form of education: first of all, be curious about something, and then really talk until you understand it, and experience it at the same time."

As is often the case with college students, Ali didn't realize what she knew and understood until she could apply the concepts to real-life situations. In this case, she talked to the girls about differences in lifestyles, about romance and sex, about the challenges that are faced. This led to some new realizations about the status of education back home.

"I became so frustrated at the mentality of most students in America. A lot of people I know have no interest in school; they are only there because they feel like they have to be, or they are following the path that everyone takes. In Nepal, going to college is a tremendous opportunity that shapes the lives of the students. Even if they don't want to go to class, they still do. They go because they don't take it for granted. Back home, students don't look at college as an amazing life opportunity; they look at it as something to do. After realizing this, I became even more upset, because these are the students who really deserve to learn, and most of the time they don't have the chance because they have so little money."

Like many others on the team, Ali reached a point of saturation where she could not take in any more. She felt overwhelmed but exhilarated, unable to process everything that she had seen and heard. The timing was perfect to switch gears, to move from the realm of the intellect to the physical. There were more challenges ahead, but these would test Ali in ways she hadn't anticipated. The trek through the Himalayas that followed taught her about self-discipline and managing pain. There was also plenty of time, walking up and down over mountain passes, to reflect on her life and the ways she has felt constricted until this point. The people she met stimulated her most of all. There was not a baby she passed that she did not hold (that is Ali on the cover of the book.) At one point on the trail, she found a baby goat (kid) lost and separated from her mother. While the group walked onward, Ali stayed behind to help the kid reunite with his wailing parent. It was this empathy and compassion that seemed to ignite with her, and burn brightly even upon her return home.

"I've been home for a while, and there has not been one day that I haven't thought about Nepal. It seems that everything I experience and learn now is different because Nepal is always in the back of my mind. I feel like I know something more, like I'm in on a secret. Now it is only a memory. I have so many mixed emotions about that. Some of the time I cry just thinking about it, because when I was there I felt more alive than I had ever felt before, and it's tough to not have that light anymore. Other times I smile and experience an overwhelming feeling of happiness. I could not be more grateful for the moments that I had, for the things that took my breath away, and for the people that I met. I experienced the secret, and that was enough for me to never forget. When I experience these emotions I think about my future. I either become very excited to go out and experience these things again in a new way, or I become upset because I don't believe I will have the chance to do so. What I am certain of for my life right now in this moment is that I have gone through something extremely special. My mind has been opened so wide that it can never go back to the way it was.

"I think it is really hard for people to think about the world in a way other than what they experience in their everyday lives. What I have experienced will never allow me to do that, and I am forever grateful. The world has so many special people and places, and everyone deserves a chance to see them. To experience another life, to really involve yourself in a new place is so refreshing. It's like you experience another form of consciousness, because you are living through something completely different than you are used to."

How can you read these words and not feel inspired to reach out to others yourself? How can you not feel a longing to dive more deeply into parts of the world that have been out of reach? How can you not want to have adventures, to have new experiences, to meet new people, and most of all, to connect with those who so desperately need your help?

Ali, and the others profiled in this chapter, report on what they *lived*, and that they had never felt so alive. Ali summarizes this best:

"My spirit has been so enriched by what I've seen, by the people I've met, by the things I've done. My heart sees clearly what I need to do next, and I'm inspired to do what I can. Each smile from a child has been a blessing for me, a reward that will last a lifetime. I have changed my mind about what is 'primitive.' In Nepal, they are so much more advanced than we are back home—especially in relationships. One of my favorite quotes is from Mother Teresa, who worked and lived in this part of the world and who reflected on what she had seen in the supposedly more advanced West: *In the developed countries there is a poverty of intimacy, a poverty of spirit, of loneliness, of lack of love. There is no greater sickness in the world today than that one.*"

⚊ ⚊

How can you read these stories and not feel inspired yourself to do something useful, especially in an environment that stimulates your senses and challenges you to learn and grow in dramatic ways? Every one of these individuals was a travel novice, inexperienced with respect to functioning within other cultures. Yes, they had enthusiasm and a certain motivation, but also they paid a price for the gains they accrued. In their own ways, each one of them experienced a period of disorientation and extreme discomfort during some stage of their helping journeys, and yet it was precisely these challenges that led to the most worthwhile and satisfying growth.

CHAPTER 8

Making Universal Connections

Cyrus is an ex-military man and counseling professor. He is a specialist in teaching cultural issues in counseling. An inner-city street kid, Cyrus was no stranger to poverty, but he was relatively sheltered from the realities of life in the third world. Cyrus was way over his head in Nepal. He struggled with the physical challenges. He was freaked out by the primitive accommodations, and refused to bathe because of the basic facilities. He refused to eat any of the local food, except for soft drinks and pizza he found in one restaurant. Yet by the time the trip was over, he was a celebrity among the children in the villages (who had never seen a black man). He was eating yak cheese and water buffalo stew with relish. Upon returning home, Cyrus changed his family life, changed the way he did his job, and took up a new cause devoted to social justice issues. He even wrote a book on the subject (Ellis & Carlson, 2008). Even more remarkably, all of this took place as a result of just 16 days spent on this project.

Who I Am

I am Cyrus Marcellus Ellis, a professor at an urban university near Chicago. I grew up as an African American male in the South, so a sense of justice was fed to me early as a young man. I heard the stories from my mother and my father concerning the march for civil rights led by Dr. King. I heard about others like Fannie Lou Haiman and Edgar Evers who stood in the face of oppression and inequality. I grew up understanding that I am someone who is part of a collective people who historically have been on the other side of fairness and justice in a lot of ways. My interest in social justice began at an early age, before I ever knew what that meant.

As I grew as a person, not just by age but by reason and understanding, I began to realize why I chose to work with the folks who usually get the short end of the stick—drug addicts, psychotics, and the homeless. Most of these people grew up in neighborhoods like me, with poor schools and few opportunities. Joining the Army was a way out for me; I joined as an enlisted man at the bottom of the ladder and eventually worked my way up to becoming an officer, serving leadership roles. In spite of my advancement and my opportunity to get a first-rate education, I have never forgotten how unfair the world is. Social justice has become for me more than just an academic term but a way of life that involves being an advocate for others without power.

What's Important, and What's Not

Prior to his trip to Nepal, Cyrus had never been outside the country, never flown on a transoceanic flight, never spent time in a foreign culture. He was an expert on multicultural issues, but his focus was on ethnic minorities within the United States. Once he boarded the plane and saw all the different people sitting next to him, all the languages spoken, he knew that he was in for something beyond his experience.

Beside the novelty of everything around him, Cyrus also struggled with leaving his family behind. He had never left his children before for more than a few days. He was going through some personal issues that were weighing on his mind, as well as some challenges at work. Yet he admits this was the best time for him to get away, to not only go toward something completely new, but also to get away from what was most familiar.

"This trip really made me take a hard look at life," Cyrus admits with a laugh. "Not just my life, but life in general. It made me look at what's most important, and what's not so important."

Cyrus was particularly surprised by how people who have so little can still manage to enjoy their lives in ways he had not seen before. He had known his own poverty and deprivation as a child, as well as oppression, but it was on a scale that was different from what he was encountering in Nepal.

"These people don't have a thing. They don't have toilets or shoes or lights. There's this line that came to mind from a Bruce Lee movie called *Enter the Dragon*. This karate guy has to go to Hong Kong to fight in this tournament. He was looking around and seeing the way people live in the squalor of the city and said something I'll never forget: 'Ghettos are the same all over the world. They stink.'

"Now where we were wasn't exactly a ghetto, but it qualifies as the worst poverty I've ever seen. I mean, people survive on a few hundred dollars per *year*. I know in America there are places that are rough, but not like this. I was walking around the city and I really began to look at the people face-to-face, not just through the window of a passing car. Of course they looked at me too, this six-foot-four big black guy—they don't have too many of us in that part of the world. I remember seeing the way the women carried their babies on their backs because strollers and those kinds of things aren't really there. They'd be carrying their babies all the while they're sweeping or selling fruit. Life is hard, really hard. But I never saw any fights or disagreements. No car accidents, which is really amazing if you see the way they drive. Nobody yells at anyone or honks their horn in anger."

Of course there was a civil war going on for the previous six years, with thousands of innocent people murdered, not to mention many more casualties among the armed forces and rebels. But those battles take place in the countryside, shielded from tourist eyes. The point is that the Nepalese have the same potential to commit acts of violence as do people anywhere else in the world, but such behavior is not part of normal social behavior where a degree of cooperation is absolutely required for the infrastructure to function even minimally. As one Nepalese companion commented, shaking his head at the chaotic traffic congestion in Kathmandu: "We have many rules here, but nobody pays attention to them."

In Cyrus's words, "There is something about the people that allows them to endure. I think I know what resilience is, I think I understand what it means to be patient—but there is something different about these people that I've never seen before, nor seen since. That's one of the things that happens, going abroad and working with people from a different culture—discovering unique human qualities.

"Right now, I look at some things I brought home, things that sit in my office—a statue of Buddha, a rock, some Tibetan chimes—and they remind me of the tranquility that I witnessed there. There is something inside them that I haven't seen in my lifetime, although I've heard stories in my family's folklore that there once was a time when my race had *it*, whatever that is. Hearing about *it* is one thing, but seeing *it* is another. Maybe that was a point of connection for me while I was there, because I could see the inequitable circumstances of life that they lived with. I could see the things they do to make a dollar, or a rupee. I saw young kids working and women bearing a heavy burden and I saw men doing what they have to do to make it."

CUTTING LOOSE

Cyrus stares at his artifacts, a lost look in his eyes as he travels back in time to his visit in Nepal. He remembers the wonderful people he met, the openness of those

120

he talked to, their wonder and curiosity about him, their warmth and kindness. He struggles to find words to describe what still endures for him and decides that he can best sum things up in a few stories.

"We took this small plane to an airport that was nothing more than a runway in the middle of nowhere. It was like those movies you see where the soldiers or missionaries get off the plane and just start walking—that's just what we did, since there was no transportation or anything. The good news is that the hotel bathroom was cleaner than the one in Kathmandu, so that was a relief.

"After settling in, we drove about an hour on this bumpy road, really not much of a road at all, to this village where we got out and started walking. Then I saw this crowd of people waiting for us, lined up on both sides of the road. They literally showered us with flowers as a form of greeting. I remember all the kids and everyone touching me and looking so happy to see us.

"These people really have so little. They don't have wood to build a fire at night. They don't have clean water. Their animals, like their water buffalos and goats, live right in their homes—if you can call them that. The kids don't have shoes and their clothes are old and torn. Yet they all opened their arms and hearts to us.

"Pretty soon, we were completely surrounded by everyone in the village, and I was getting a lot of attention because clearly I am the biggest, tallest, darkest dude they've ever seen. I was, like, a foot taller than most of the others around me."

Cyrus was flattered and uncomfortable by all the attention and was unsure what to make of what he was seeing and experiencing, which was quite unlike anything he'd ever encountered before. Music started playing, followed by speeches, and then a celebration dance in which everyone was jumping around roughly in time to the beat. Cyrus was mostly hanging back, watching the show with an amused grin on his face.

"This little, older woman came and grabbed my hand and pulled me into the circle. I must tell you that I was taken aback; I certainly was appreciative and I really did not know what to do, but when in Nepal, do as the Nepalese do. I began to engage with them. We could not speak, at least in verbal language. But we were dancing, Indian style, with our hands moving, laughing and playing. I could see all the other women laughing and pointing at me and I don't know if they thought I was funny or cute or some kind of freak, but by that time I didn't care—I was cutting loose."

I Carry this Moment Forever

After his initial apprehensions had vanished, Cyrus began to dance with everyone in the circle. When the time came to leave, he felt disappointed that there wouldn't be more of an opportunity to hang out with the people. Reluctantly, he pulled himself away, waving to everyone, thanking people for their warm hospitality.

"I started walking back down the road toward our vehicle when I felt something at my side. I looked down and saw this tiny little girl in her school uniform. She couldn't have been more than seven years old. And she reached out shyly and grabbed my hand, holding on tight. I wasn't sure what I was supposed to do at this point. Was I breaking some cultural taboo? I tried to pull away a little but the girl was holding on tight, so tight I couldn't jerk away. So I just kept walking while I looked down at her. It was like she was holding on to me for dear life.

"We walked for several minutes down that path, holding hands, not saying one word to one another. I don't even speak one semicolon of the language, much less a word. But we were holding on to one another, this beautiful little girl who obviously had some kind of attachment to me. I smiled at this little girl and my heart started to really open up as she was looking into my eyes. It began to hit me that I was half a world away from what I know and what I understand. All I had done was come over here to bring some school supplies and try to help a few girls not get caught up in the sex trade industry of India. Maybe I had done more than I thought. I began to feel this universal connection with all people through this little girl."

Cyrus felt uncomfortable with the intimacy developed in such a short time with a little girl from a different world. He wondered what it was about him that the girl gravitated to. Was it the novelty of his size? Was it is black skin? Or was it something about him that she sensed or felt? Whatever it was, Cyrus felt an almost spiritual connection to the girl, to her people, and to the world, even though he was at a loss to describe this feeling. He was just so moved by the graciousness of the people, their warmth and openness, even though they had so little to give. During visits to the children's homes, Cyrus was offered a cup of tea or a small orange, about all the families had to offer. Everywhere he went, he was greeted with a welcoming and sincere, "Namaste."

"I was beginning to feel sad as we approached the van to take us back to our hotel. I knew I was about to let go of this little girl's hand and I wanted to hold on to her as hard as she was gripping me. I knew I would probably never see her again. I didn't even know her name. I didn't know what I wanted to say to her, even if I could say it. So many things were going through my heart and my head. I just felt such love from the girl and all the people. This was a powerful thing for me, maybe one of the most powerful experiences of my life.

"I turned toward the girl and just looked at her. I didn't know what to say, how to express what I was feeling, so I just blurted out, "thank you." I didn't know what else to do. The girl just looked at me, nodded her head, and smiled. I don't know what made me do it, but I took this necklace with a medallion from around my neck. It was an American eagle that reminds me of my time in the army as commander of a company. My call sign was 'Eagle 6,' my name during radio communications, so I always carry an eagle with me for luck. During the previous weeks, I had held the eagle medallion to give me support when the walking was hard or I was freaked out about something. It meant a lot to me because of the all the memories I associate with service to my country.

"Looking down at this young girl, I felt her innocence and her purity, and most of all, her vulnerability. I had to do something to protect her. So I took the necklace off my neck and pointed to her, miming that it was a gift for her. I put it carefully around her neck and said to her with total sincerity, 'This is for you. This is yours now.'"

"The smile on that girl's face couldn't be believed. All her friends, who had been watching us, ran up to examine her new gift. They were laughing and giggling but the girl, though proud, kept touching it and looking at it, then looking back at me. This was one of the most beautiful sights I have ever seen in my life. It was so pure and sweet and genuine."

With sadness and regret, Cyrus climbed inside the van, fighting back tears. Cyrus is a tough guy, an ex-soldier and warrior, who still maintains the stature of his training. Yet he felt himself melting. He took a few deep breaths and settled himself in the seat, prepared to re-enter the world he had left behind.

The van started to pull away when someone cried out to him, "Cyrus, Cyrus, look behind you."

Sure enough, the little girl had run up to the van and was underneath Cyrus's window, standing on her tiptoes. Cyrus turned and looked down at her, wondering what she wanted to say. She signaled for him to open the window.

"I didn't know what she could possibly say to me, not speaking any English, or what I could say to her, but I leaned out the window anyway. The little girl stretched herself as far as she could—and then kissed me on the cheek. She started giggling and then ran off toward her friends. I was just floored, smiling and giggling myself. I just can't tell you what this meant to me. I've thought over and over how I wish I could hit the reset button and live that moment again and again as it was one of the most special things in my life. I carry that moment inside me every day."

CHAPTER 9

Lessons and Major Themes

Each of the stories presented in previous chapters, as well as the ones that follow, illustrate the ways that well-meaning people—students, professors, tradesmen, and professionals—not only volunteered their time to raise money for a cause dear to their hearts, but also delivered themselves to the villages so they could act as witnesses to what their efforts achieved. While inspiration is indeed important, it is just as critical that we next turn our attention to action.

We are about to broaden the scope of our discussion, moving from one specific project to several other social justice efforts that are underway in a variety of settings and with diverse missions. These projects demonstrate the range of possibilities that await you and highlight all the ways that you can make a difference. Before we expand upon the ways that social justice projects can be initiated and promoted, we'd like to synthesize some of the themes that have been evident thus far. This chapter brings together some of the most important lessons that may have bearing on your own future efforts.

SOME UNIVERSAL FACTORS

At the beginning of the story of his experiences building schools in remote areas of Pakistan and Afghanistan, Greg Mortenson (Mortenson & Relin, 2006) made an initial impulsive gesture to assist members of a village who saved his life after he became lost during an expedition to climb K2, the most challenging Himalayan peak in the world. As with our Nepal project, which developed from a similar spontaneous action, Mortenson found that his initial dabbling as a do-gooder began to take over his life. He surrendered nearly all worldly possessions, donated all his money and salary to fund his project, and spent months at a time living in isolated villages where he became fluent in local dialects and became proficient in cultural practices. He survived a kidnapping by the Taliban, a *fatwa* (death sentence) from a jealous *mullah*, corruption and deception by local agents he trusted, and unimaginable hardships living under the same deprived conditions as the people he was helping.

With all the money Mortenson eventually raised to build more than hundred schools throughout central Asia, and all the projects he undertook to expand his efforts (initiating recycling programs, digging wells, providing medical care, building latrines and wells, augmenting teacher salaries), he still insisted that he gained as much as the villagers he was helping. When Sir Edmund Hillary wanted to repay the Sherpas for their help in supporting his climb of Everest, one of the village elders responded with great sincerity and respect that perhaps Hillary and his culture had little to offer them, especially with regard to courage, strength, and resilience. "And we don't envy your restless spirit," Urkien Sherpa said. "But we would like our children to go to school. Of all the things you have, learning is the one we most desire for our children" (Hillary, 1964).

In the case of Mortensen and the people profiled in earlier chapters, as well as those who follow, several personal benefits were described and enjoyed by the participants. Many of these narratives are consistent with some of the research that has been done on the transformative properties of such helping experiences (Brown & Lehto, 2005; Dukes, 2006; Ferruci, 2006; Little & Schmidt, 2006; Wilson & Harris, 2006).

1. *Greater simplicity.* Participants have mentioned repeatedly that they felt a significant impact seeing people who appear to have so little and yet display greater levels of life satisfaction and happiness then those back home. In many cases, this led team members to simplify their lives once they returned, to reduce their consumption of material goods, and to concentrate on the things that mattered most to them. They often learned that they could live happily on less, much less, and instead devote resources to the things that mattered most.

2. *Changed values.* Participants observed that, as in many other developing countries, the Nepalese culture emphasizes family connections and relationships

among all else. It was jarring to both witness and experience a slower pace of life that emphasized living in the moment instead of being concerned with ambitions and future plans. Although this is a powerful insight, it is an ideal that is great in theory but difficult to put into practice over the long haul. Most of us are easily seduced by the work and hectic schedules that seem to take over our lives.

3. *Resilience and confidence related to facing adversity.* During the most recent trip, there was almost never a moment when someone wasn't crying or on the verge of tears. This sort of emotional upheaval is not only commonplace but to be expected during times when you are overwhelmed. Several people had to deal with physical challenges that seemed beyond them, such as climbing up endless stairs cut into the side of a mountain or crossing rickety bridges that were held together with spit. Others struggled with physical discomforts, such as squat toilets, illnesses, or dicey living quarters. Almost everyone suffered emotionally while being so close to poverty and deprivation. Yet it is true that what doesn't destroy you makes you stronger; volunteers return to their worlds far better prepared to deal with annoyances, discomforts, and challenges that arise.

4. *Constructive guilt and shame about being privileged.* When you see people barely surviving with so little at their disposal—eating one meal a day, living in a mud-floor hut, walking around without shoes, coping with rampant disease and malnutrition—it can't help but penetrate the shell of any close observer. One of the common effects is feeling guilty because, relatively speaking, we have so much more. This is a normal reaction to confronting inequity; it can also be constructive in encouraging each of us to examine what we have and feel more appreciative of these opportunities. It may also act as a motivation to do more in the future to help those who are marginalized.

5. *Enhanced social interest and support.* Community involvement in almost any capacity means functioning as part of a supportive group working together as a team. Studies have demonstrated that students who volunteer as part of a larger group significantly decrease their likelihood of engaging in self-destructive addictions like binge drinking. They are also able to develop greater compassion and empathy for others, making them better equipped in the future to experience intimacy in their relationships.

Every transformative experience has bridges to cross and obstacles to negotiate along the way. A student with an intense fear of heights is pictured here crossing a dubious structure that resembles a bridge.

6. *Exhilaration and joy.* Human beings are among the few species on the planet that will sacrifice their time, resources, and even lives to help others who are not genetically related (Flora, 2008). Our altruistic spirit is partially what drives us to devote significant energy to assist those who are misfortunate enough to lack the basic means to survive. It is a basic premise of this book, and the stories contained therein, that volunteers and "do-gooders" experience a kind of euphoria, if not spiritual transcendence, as a result of their efforts.

7. *Creating meaning.* One of the things that most contributes to any experience having an enduring effect is the meaning-making that occurs during and after the events. Volunteer and service activities are much more likely to have lasting influence when the participants invest the time reflecting

Some of the volunteers hanging out with local students in the village, exchanging ideas and comparing notes about their lifestyles.

and talking about what it all meant to them. In many cases, such analysis has led to dramatic life changes that persist until this day.

Specific to the project in Nepal, there are also some important lessons that the people and place offered to participants. First and foremost was appreciating living in the moment. So many of us live our lives obsessed with planning for the future. We have our schedules booked days, even weeks or months in advance. We fantasize about future dreams and aspirations. We think constantly about what might lie over the next horizon. Yet volunteers to Nepal and many other developing countries are impacted strongly by exposure to a place where people live very much in the present. Rather than hurrying off to the next big thing, rushing to the next appointment, answering phones to interrupt conversations, people make time to be with one another in ways that we don't often see within our own world. Witnessing these interactions inspired students to spend more focused time with their own family and friends once they returned home. Alas, even with the best of intentions, modern life intrudes and makes its demands known.

Namaste: Honoring the Spirit of the "Other"

I just couldn't believe the way everyone takes time to greet us on the road or anywhere in the villages. Old people, young people, everyone smiles, cups their hands into a triangle under their chin, and says "Namaste" with total reverence and respect. There is no exact translation in English but I think it means something along the lines of, "My spirit honors the divine within you." [Laughs] Hey, for all I know it could just mean, "Screw you, imperialist invader," but I don't think so.

It is such a lovely custom, that even strangers are greeted with caring and respect. I remember walking through this one pathway and this little girl, who couldn't have been more than two years old, held up her hands and said in that little sing-song voice, "Namaste." It just gives me the shivers to remember that.

I've been trying to introduce this to some of my friends. They make fun of me, but I think they get a kick out of it.

OVERCOMING FUTILITY AND FRUSTRATION

The reality of working on service projects is that your sense of hope and faith will be vigorously tested. Nick Heil, a mountaineer and guide who has devoted considerable efforts toward improving the safety and security of local people in the Himalayas, admits that although he has made a bit of a difference, it really may not matter all that much. "But life's like a bucket of water—you put your hand in it, and shake your hand around, and it makes a few waves. Then you take your hand out, and nothing's changed" (Brice, 2008, p. 122).

Such an attitude may represent false modesty or perhaps a pessimistic view of one's own relative insignificance, but it seems to us that it can lead to feelings of discouragement and futility. Why invest so much of yourself in helping others if, in your heart, you don't genuinely believe that it will make some kind of lasting difference, even a small ripple in the water—a drop in the bucket, so to speak?

CHALLENGES OF SUSTAINED COMMITMENT

It is a common scenario: students volunteer for a cause, put in their time, do what they can for a semester or two, and then move on to the next thing that strikes their fancy, leaving it to others to carry on the work. It's no big deal; you were only one small cog in the bureaucratic machine. You'll have fond (or perhaps trying) memories of your experience, the brief stint helping others. It is kind of the way that some people think of their military service—an interesting adventure, doing something useful, but after a short while, it's time to move on to real life.

I (Jeffrey) have been doing service learning trips for many years, taking a dozen or more students and educators to meet with children in the villages. The participants are usually moved to tears by the poverty and deprivation they witness, as well as by their noble efforts to be helpful. You have been a witness to their journeys in previous chapters. They talk a lot about how important and wonderful this sort of work is and how honored they feel to be part of the effort. They feel like they have made a difference, one that even might have been a highlight of their lives. "I've never felt so alive," one student commented. "I really think what we went through is what life is all about, seeing the world as it is, being kind, helping others along the way. It is hard to leave all that and come back home."

Yet I have been surprised by how few of the participants ever follow through on their intentions once they return home. They jump right back into the material world of consumption, seeking success and wealth. I never hear from the vast majority of people again. That is not to say, of course, that they haven't moved on to bigger and better things, just that sustained commitment in a social justice cause is somewhat rare.

The truth of the matter, when all is said and done, is that good intentions are not nearly enough. It is noble and worthy to say you want to make the world a better place, to help the needy who are in no position to help themselves. It is even more honorable to take those first, small steps to volunteer your time to a cause that touches your heart, or to enter a profession in which you do this for a living. But it takes a heck of a lot more commitment to sustain the effort over time. Very few individuals can—or want—to do this.

People often make one impulsive gesture from the heart and then lose interest and go on to the next challenge. The effects of such well intended but brief efforts can be devastating. What, then, if you take a step forward from which there is no turning back, no abandonment possible? What if you make a promise to a child or a village, one that must be kept at all costs?

And so it is that I (Jeffrey) find myself committed to a cause throughout the balance of my life. It doesn't feel like I have an option to change my mind, to move on to something else; there are too many lives at stake. And yet there are few experiences in life more fulfilling than not only doing something "good," but sticking around long enough to see the fruits of your efforts.

I have been a therapist most of my life, and I've said before how it can be extremely frustrating not to know if and when I've ever made a difference. Clients lie. They say they are feeling better when they are actually feeling worse. They report no progress when, in fact, things may actually be significantly better. Most of the time, people just go away after I've seen them and I never hear what happened afterwards. Even more frustrating, the people I've seen often come with long-term, severe, intractable problems that take months—if not years—to resolve.

A part of me has always wanted to be a car mechanic. They diagnose a problem, pull out the worn part, replace it with a spare, and in an hour they've (hopefully) got the thing running again. They even supply invoices that list how much time it took them and a list of parts that were used. Most of the time, I'm not even sure what the "real" problem is that people bring me, and there is even less certainty about what it was that I said or did that was most helpful. As a therapist, and a teacher, I live in a world of ambiguity and mystery, doing my best to influence people but never quite sure what I do that matters most. On top of that, I'm impatient. Yet now, I feel the burden and responsibility of a long-term commitment that I can never abandon. Even Moses never saw the Promised Land.

As we move into the action part of the content, highlighting options that you might consider in your own helping journey, we want to bring into clear focus that this is serious business, not just something you do to beef up your resume or jump into as an adventure. A bit later, we will highlight the tremendous personal benefits that accrue to those who choose an altruistic path; however, we also want to remind you that there are indeed other lives at stake and other causes far more significant than your own personal agenda.

BEING THE LONELY ONE

One student who worked in one of the villages we support left her home in Norway for a "gap" year to volunteer before she started her university studies. Marie arrived in Nepal eager to do something useful. She was put to work teaching in the local school.

"I am a girl from Norway," Marie introduces herself with modesty and a certain reticence. "I come from a family with five girls, as well as my mother and father. So I have always learned how to stand on my own two feet. Since we are a big family, and both my parents work a lot, I have been finding and running my own projects based on what I want to do."

When Marie was 11 years old, she spent a summer with other children from 12 different countries, igniting in her a strong interest in global affairs and diverse cultures. She arranged student exchanges for herself during high school (to Italy and Germany), lived with families, and learned the local languages (in addition to her fluency in Norwegian and English). She also volunteered her time throughout high school to work with needy children, both in her own country and elsewhere. In other words, Marie was quite worldly and a veteran of many youth service organizations.

After graduating high school, Marie didn't know what she wanted to do with her life. It wasn't a lack of available opportunities as much as feeling overwhelmed with all the possibilities and her varied interests. Unlike American students, who are eager to go to college and join the high-pressure corporate world, many European young women (and men) take a year off to travel, see the world, and often volunteer working for some cause. Marie had worked just long enough to save enough money for her to live in basic survival mode in a developing country.

"Today is my last day here, after one year," Marie told us. "Now I am looking back on what I have done and what I have seen." Rather than feeling only pride and exhilaration in what she has accomplished working with the children for a year, Marie is sober and serious in her assessment of what she has done.

"Being here in Nepal has been a big culture shock for me, even with the other places I have lived. People talk to one another differently than what I am used to. They love their boys here, but not so much their girls. There are bad things that happen here but there are no police to stop them."

Marie wouldn't go into much detail about what she has witnessed, but she had been living in a center of Maoist revolution during the civil war, where people have been killed, where girls have disappeared, where neighbors have turned against one another because of their different castes and political beliefs.

"I have learned a lot about when to be quiet. In Norway, I can tell others what I think and what I feel. But here I have not been able to do that, especially because I am only a girl. They expect me to be quiet and obedient."

Marie could hardly contain her indignation and anger over the ways that some local people behaved towards her and others. She resented the laziness and complacency that she saw, at least from her point of view, in some teachers who did not do their jobs or even show up for work. She wondered why she was working so hard to make the place better when she felt so alone in her efforts; others didn't seem to care at all.

Marie acknowledged that even after a year of living in her village, she still did not understand much of what went on around her. "I am not here to change their culture. I am not here to tell them what I think they are doing wrong. But it is so difficult to stand by and watch the way things fall apart. I ask myself over and over again, every day, why am I here? What good have I done?"

Marie was very hard on herself. In the year she lived in Nepal she had learned to speak the language. As she walked throughout the village, children came running to grab her hand, give her a hug, and tell her about their day. She smiled as she thought about the children, but such moments of joy were fleeting. "I feel lonely so much of the time," Marie admitted, "and I am so very frustrated!"

Any students who wants to volunteer must have a realistic view of what they can actually accomplish in such a short period of time. Marie shook her head at the prospect of spending only a few weeks, or a few months, working somewhere. Even after a year, she doubted whether anything she has done would have a lasting effect after she left.

"I am just so tired now, so discouraged. I am sorry to talk this way, but this is the way it has been for me."

Marie with two of the children she was teaching.

Remember, that was Marie's last day of her yearlong service. She was home-sick and anxious to return to Norway. She had expected that this assignment would be a lot easier than it had been, that everyone would welcome her with grateful arms and thank her repeatedly for her noble efforts. The reality was that she was often caught in political and social struggles she barely under-stood, much less could negotiate effectively.

In spite of her discouragement on this day, her last one abroad, Marie felt a renewed commitment to studying world cultures. She thought that she would study social anthropology when she gets to college, or maybe international politics. She was driven, more than ever before, to make sense of the ways that people live and operate in the world.

"I have been travelling a lot in my life, and lived in many families for several weeks, but during this trip I have been living with a Nepalese family for a long time. This has helped me to better understand the community. In the West, we have a strong belief that we know what is right and best and so on. But that is the problem with organizations trying to help people in places where they don't really understand what is going on and what the real problems might be."

This is a profound statement, and one that is critical for students who really want to understand the way the world works. There is only so much you can learn in the classroom or from books like this one. There is just no substitute for the kind of learning that takes place deep within the community, when you are actually accepted as part of the community.

Even though she was only 19, Marie now had the confidence that she really "knew" things that most people will never understand. She felt proud of what she has discovered. "People like to spin around one story and make it bigger than it is, but I can tell what I have seen. Since I had to be a part of their culture, I learned a lot about their traditions and had to just learn how they do it. In Norway I helped my friends from Kosovo and Somalia get to know the Norwegian culture, but it is totally different to be 'the lonely one.' It is very difficult to learn a new language and culture. But I think it has taught me a lot."

Looking back on her year's journey and devotion to the community in rural Nepal, struggling with her feelings of loneliness and alienation, her frustrations and sense of futility, Marie still concluded on a hopeful note.

"The children have been part of a forgotten people for many generations. They have been the poorest, with few opportunities, and have been treated like animals. Fortunately, their situation can—and will—change with help and support. They need education most of all. This won't happen overnight but through small, incremental steps. Education will help the children and their families feel respected. It is possible to show the children that they should work hard in school even though they are poor. Even if, one day, you forget them, they will never forget you and what you have done to give them hope for the future."

Marie's story of showing up alone in a village, spending a year there to learn the language and culture, and do what she can to help the children, is a testament to her courage and determination to make some kind of difference. Even with her frustrations and doubts, when all is said and done, she knew in her heart that she had done something useful, something that would sustain her as she continued her own education.

In spite of her claims to the contrary, we have plenty of evidence—and testimonials—that Marie did, in fact, have a huge impact on the lives of the children and their families. It is now two years later, and people in the community still talk about Marie as if she is still present among them. Although she was only just out of high school, she exuded a sense of assurance and compassion that villages found both attractive and engaging. They appreciated that Marie listened to them without interrupting the way Westerners are so often inclined to do. And when she responded, Marie did so with unusual sensitivity and respect.

There had been other volunteer students in the village, but very few ever took the time, or invested the hard work, in learning the local language. The villagers liked the way that Marie didn't seem to judge them or their way of life, even though they were so very poor. They offered the best complement of all: Marie seemed to be one of them, rather than a stranger.

What was it that Marie managed to apply in her work that might be instructive for anyone else who wanted to have a similar impact? Even though she was neither professionally trained nor particularly experienced, Marie understood intuitively that to have any kind of influence she would first have to earn the villagers' respect. She applied some fairly basic relationship skills that allowed her to listen with caring and compassion—and to respond appropriately in such a way that she was heard.

The following chapter introduces some of the basic skills that Marie found so helpful in her work and that are a crucial part of any helping relationship—whether in social work, commerce, education, health services, counseling, or any other profession.

PART III

Taking Action

CHAPTER 10

Relationship Skills for Promoting Constructive Action

High motivation and deliberate intention will carry you a long way toward helping people, but they are hardly enough unless you have sufficient training and skills to implement your plans. There is nothing more dangerous than do-gooders with the best of intentions who blithely jump into situations that they don't understand. The first rule of medicine, that applies equally to any helping effort, is to *do no harm*. More often than not, serious damage occurs not through deliberate hurtful acts, but rather through ignorance.

It is beyond the scope of a single chapter or even a single book to teach you everything that you need to know to enter into a new culture and help to implement helpful programs. It often takes advanced degrees, years of training on the job, and lots of experience and supervision to reach the point where you feel anything near prepared. Yet if you stay within your limits and concentrate on a few modest goals, you can do a lot of good with minimal preparation. This is especially the case if you have learned basic relationship skills that are most useful in helping situations.

Your college offers many courses on helping skills, which include strategies to use with individuals, groups, organizations, and families to deal with a variety of problems. In the material that follows, we review some of the basics that will serve you well not only in volunteer assignments and work settings, but in all your relationships that matter most. These skills will help you to be a better listener, a more compassionate and empathic responder, and a more sensitive and caring human being. Although it usually takes three years of graduate school to learn these skills well enough to perform at a professional level, there are basic methods that you can start using right away, and you will notice immediate results in all your conversations with others. This is not magic we are introducing, but rather some very important ideas that most people are not familiar with, or at least don't apply very regularly.

As just one example, consider how rare it is that you ever have (or give) undivided attention to someone during a typical conversation. Often, you are distracted or multitasking, doing several things at the same time. Or notice how often you are involved in some important discussion and, when a cell phone rings, you or someone else stops the conversation to answer the call. What exactly does this communicate? It says that no matter what we are doing right now, and how important it might be, it is not nearly as important as whatever is waiting on the other end of this phone. The same is true during all the times you are talking to someone while at the same time doing something else—reading papers, waving to someone, fumbling with your stuff, thinking about things you will do later. You're essentially communicating to others that although you are interested in what they are saying, you aren't *so* interested that you are willing to stop doing a dozen other things at the same time. Among all the things we will mention in this section, the single most significant point—one that is very easy to learn but very difficult to practice—is getting in the habit of attending fully and completely during helping encounters.

WORKING WITHIN OTHER CULTURES

Other cultures do not only exist in exotic faraway countries, but in *any* setting in which the customs, rituals, and context are different from what you are used to. Corporations have particular cultures, as do geographic regions, small towns and big cities, professions and leisure activities. Whether you are a snowboarder, surfer, chess player, engineering major, video gamer, or have any of a thousand other interests, you speak your own language and share values similar to others who are identified strongly with this group. To be helpful within this group or any other culture, you must have some working knowledge of the setting that you are entering, including familiarization with language, customs, and expected behavior.

There are places in the world where you would never want to greet anyone with your left hand, or touch someone's head, or make direct eye contact, or sit on the floor, or wear your shoes inside, or talk about anything other than the weather for the first few minutes of a meeting. Of course, it helps to study the culture ahead of time, as well as to talk with people who have been to where you are going, but you will also want to be cautious and careful until you learn what is expected and how to behave appropriately. We are not talking about going just to places like the Congo, Bangladesh, or Uruguay, but to any locale where you have little experience. Expected behavior in New York is quite different than New Orleans, Louisiana; Jackson, Mississippi; Los Angeles, California; or Fargo, North Dakota. This may seem rather obvious, but as you are an outsider, initial reactions to you will often be cautious, if not mistrustful.

It is critical that you examine and confront your own cultural perceptions and biases. Based on your own background, privileged in some ways but certainly slanted in others, you have rather strong beliefs about what is good, what is right, what is best, and what is desirable for everyone. Yet people in other places live by different rules and customs that reflect their own values and preferences as well as their unique situations.

There will be many times when you catch yourself making critical judgments about the way people behave around you. Sometimes you will say these aloud, but most of the time you will think silently: "I can't believe that they do that!" "What is wrong with these people?" "Why do they act that way?" Most of the time, these are variations of a main theme: "Why aren't these people more like me and what I am used to?"

To help people, to be welcomed and trusted by them, you must be able to enter their worlds without such judgments. If they sense your scorn or pity, you will lose their confidence in your ability to help them. It often helps to approach such situations with a completely open mind, one in which you fully expect that you are the learner and they are your teachers. Regardless of what you think you already know and understand, assume that any influence that takes place in your relationships will be reciprocal.

Consider that anything you do to help should occur with tremendous sensitivity to the particular cultural context in which you are operating. As one example, in our own project we focus on helping lower-caste girls, children who are ordinarily treated as less than worthless, a drain on resources in the

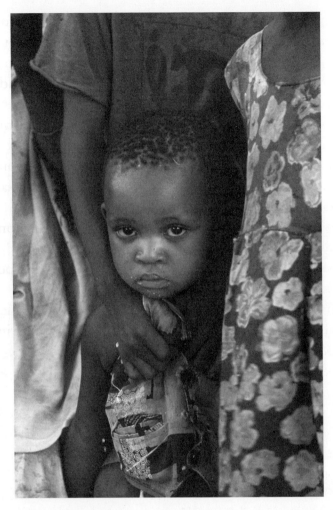

In spite of your good intentions and enthusiasm, it takes a while to develop trust with those you are helping.

village. Our project occurs within a culture in which women and girls are marginalized and rarely offered opportunities for education and advancement. And here come these strangers from abroad and select (with the principal's and teachers' assistance) girls who may be academically talented, but who come from "untouchable" families. We may believe that we are helping those who need it the most, but to elders and leaders in the village, we are going against their customs. Why aren't we helping the boys from the Brahmin caste? Why aren't we buying land for them and building them schools?

We explained our narrow mission, but it just didn't make sense to them. And when you think about it from their perspective, how could it? We were at a stalemate, because neither the villagers nor us really grasped each other's perspective; if we couldn't reach some accommodation and mutual understanding, then further collaboration would fall apart. We couldn't speak with authority about what "they" were thinking, but our own internal thoughts were highly judgmental ("This is *so* primitive") and resentful ("What is wrong with these people and why don't they appreciate all that we are doing for them?"). It is highly likely that they were thinking something similar about us.

There was a crisis on our hands that could only be resolved if we looked at things from one another's point of view, if we found common ground in our strategies. Somehow, we had to negotiate a compromise that satisfied our goals and yet continued to secure the cooperation of the village power structure; without that, our efforts would be sabotaged.

The particular solution to this problem doesn't really matter (we ended up providing some supplies and resources for all the children in the school) as much as the approach we had to take to resolve the conflict. Unless we could make adjustments to satisfy those with power (the older male elders), appreciating and honoring their values, we would remain at a stalemate. Of course, we also had to figure out a way to honor our own primary mission.

LISTENING SKILLS

Although we are talking about skills that are intended to be used in helping situations, you will find these techniques of immeasurable value in all your interactions with others. In fact, the best way to learn these skills and integrate them as part of your normal interpersonal style is to practice them as often as you can with everyone you meet. These are the same techniques that psychotherapists and counselors use to build collaborative relationships with clients, since they are intended to create trust and intimacy in the most efficient way.

At the simplest level, before you can help anyone, you first have to learn to listen, as we illustrated with Marie's efforts in the previous chapter. Surprisingly, most people don't do that very well. By listening, we mean giving undivided, focused attention to those with whom you are speaking, communicating intent interest in a natural and caring way. In our culture, this usually means direct eye contact, appropriate head nods to indicate you are following, and responses that reflect what you've heard and understood. In other cultures, adaptations are needed according to local norms. For instance, in some cultures direct eye contact could be viewed as distrustful, if not aggressive (think of inner city gangs, for instance).

Step 1: Before You Begin. The first thing you must do in any helping interaction is to prepare yourself so that you can devote full attention to the encounter. This means resisting all other distractions, focusing your concentration, and clearing your mind so you can take in all that you hear, sense, and observe. It also means closely monitoring the critical voice within you, the one that constantly judges other people according to your standards. You want to attain a state of calmness, acceptance, openness, and compassion. In one sense, this requires a kind of meditative trance in which you keep bringing your attention to the present every time it wanders off track. Before you can do this, you first have to make a commitment that you are willing to invest the energy it takes to remain deeply engaged with others.

Step 2: Positioning. Use your body and physical space to best communicate your interest and hovering attention. This usually involves facing the person fully, putting aside all other tasks (papers, cell phone, camera, etc.), and sitting at an appropriate distance that is both comfortable and unobtrusive. Depending on the person's age, gender, and cultural context, this space can be arranged in a number of different ways. In one situation, you might sit next to the person, holding his or her hand; in another situation, you might sit across from the person at a respectful distance. Regardless of the situation, you will want to position yourself to communicate respect and interest.

Step 3: Responding. We are not talking about responding verbally quite yet, but rather listening actively. You do this nonverbally through body posture and gestures such as nodding your head. You communicate your interest and understanding through appropriate facial expressions (smiles, frowns, concern). Remember, you haven't spoken yet—we haven't gotten that far. You are listening with all your being, listening with caring and empathy, listening with respect. You would be amazed how healing this can be for people, even if you do nothing else.

RESPONDING

It isn't your job to fix problems but to empower people to do so for themselves. This takes a certain amount of pressure off you, since your role is to facilitate progress rather than to make it happen yourself. Since you will likely work as part of a team, hopefully there is shared responsibility for the desired outcome.

Now that you have listened carefully and sensitively to what has been said, your responses can be formulated in such a way that you reflect back what you've heard. This approach can focus on both the content of the message as well as its underlying meaning and the person's feelings. In the conversation on the next page, note how the helper uses 1) *paraphrases* that reflect the *content* of what has been said, and 2) *reflections of feeling* to highlight the *emotions* associated with those messages.

Comparing Worlds

I saw these people living in such squalor. My God, their toilets were just a hole in the ground. There were, like, eight people living in a room the size of my bedroom at home, all sleeping on the dirt floor. They had no lights, no electricity. All they had to eat each day were a few bowls of rice and this watery lentil soup, plus a lot of tea to fill their bellies. I gotta tell you, at first I was disgusted. I'm embarrassed to admit this but I thought they were like animals, like these goats they had tethered out back. I thought, "There's no way I can work with these people; they're just too different from me." But then I sat down with them for tea. They gave me an orange to eat. They were so proud that they had an orange to give me, their honored guest. After I sat with them for a while, and we chatted using mostly sign language and grunts and smiles, I began to realize how incredibly happy and content these people were. The children were crawling all over the place, playing with sticks and stones, wrestling a chicken. The grandparents, the parents, everyone was just so calm and peaceful. And then I started comparing them to my family and realized that these people were so much further ahead than us. I began to envy them. Soon I came to love them.

Jeffrey speaking to Madhav Ghimire, a respected poet, employing both nonverbal and verbal "attending" skills to communicate intense interest and encourage deeper conversation.

Mother: "There has been so little rain in our village. It is much worse than in prior years."

Helper: "You're concerned there won't be enough water to raise food for your family." *This paraphrase lets the mother know she has been heard and also takes the conversation deeper to the main worry.*

Mother: "We can irrigate the way we have done before. The river is full from the snows on the mountains."

Helper: "So it's not just the lack of rain that bothers you." *Note how the helper does not frame this as question but keeps reflecting back what she hears. He now realizes that the comment about the rain wasn't literal but merely an opening for the conversation.*

Mother: "That is so. We have lived many years in this place, through many such times."

Helper: "You seem worried about something else." *This simple reflection of feeling is a subtle invitation for the mother to talk about what is really bothering her. The helper has to be careful not to push too hard.*

Mother: (nods her head, then sighs) "It is my daughter."

Helper: "Your daughter Mya?" *This is a simple prompt or encouragement. Still the helper doesn't push or ask questions that could come across as too intrusive.*

Mother: "Yes, you know how she is. Very headstrong. She has too much will."

Helper: "Like her mother." *This is said gently, with a smile.*

Mother: "Oh yes. I suppose that is true. But Mya is something else. She has dreams. And these are not dreams for someone like her."

Helper: "You're worried that she is going to be disappointed by wanting something out of reach." *This is again framed as paraphrase and reflection of feeling rather than asked as a question.*

As this conversation continues, the helper is listening carefully to the concerns expressed by the mother, reflecting back what is heard, helping to clarify

Showing Respect and Kindness

Much of the time it feels like there is so little I can do to help. I am not here for that long a period of time. My contribution is just a drop in the bucket and I really wonder after I leave what difference my effort will have made. If I think about that for very long, I just feel hopeless. But then I recall the times in which my very presence in someone's home, or a conversation I've had with one of the teachers, or even playing soccer with the kids, has brought moments of such pleasure to people. It's like if I can be really and truly present with these people, honor them, treat them with kindness and respect, it helps them to feel like they really do matter. For so much of their lives they've been told they're totally worthless.

what the main issues might be. In this case, Mya dreams of leaving the village and going to university some day. Although she is an excellent student, her English skills are still weak, and nobody from their extended family has ever gone further than fifth grade (Mya is already in ninth grade). Unless Mya allows her family to arrange a marriage for her soon (she is one year past puberty), she may miss her opportunity for a husband. It is not the helper's role to give advice in this case, but to offer reassurance and support.

Although the context for this conversation is quite different from what you might normally have on campus, with your friends, or at home, the main skills are essentially universal. You give your undivided attention. You listen carefully and communicate your interest, all while you suspend critical judgment. Then you respond with compassion and caring, reflecting what you've heard. With practice and experience, this often leads to greater clarification such that people can then proceed based on new understanding. You might also consult other sources (Evans, Hearn, Uhlemann, & Ivey, 2007; Kottler, 2008) for more detailed descriptions of these methods.

RECOGNIZING DYSFUNCTIONAL THINKING PATTERNS

We include somewhat more advanced helping concepts just to introduce you to the possibilities of what you can learn in the future if you decide to devote more of your time and effort to a service profession or volunteer assignment. Without adequate fluency in a person's language and familiarity with the culture and context, it is almost impossible to identify, much less challenge, so-called dysfunctional thinking patterns that may block effective action. Nevertheless, these strategies are especially helpful when applied to your own struggles and frustrations. You can read more about cognitive therapy and rational emotive therapy techniques in some of the original sources (Beck, 2005; Dryden, 2008; Wilding & Milne, 2008).

- *Overgeneralization* takes place when you make an erroneous assumption, based on a single case, assuming that something is always true. "Because this guy won't cooperate with my plans, nobody else will either."

- *Personalization* involves exaggerating the extent that events in the world apply to yourself. "Every time I try something, it *never* works out."
- *Dichotomous thinking* means dividing things into extreme categories. "Either I get the job and become destined for greatness, or lose the opportunity and become destined for mediocrity."
- *Mind reading* represents a kind of arbitrary inference, in which you assume that you know what others are thinking. These conclusions are generally not supported by objective facts. "I can tell that the leader doesn't like me because he ignored the question I asked him."
- *Awfulizing* takes place when you exaggerate the level of discomfort or inconvenience that you are experiencing. "It is *terrible* that we have to deal with this traffic congestion and such a *disaster* that we will be late to the meeting."
- *Absolute demands* involve expectations that you should get what you want and it is awful when you don't (see above). This can also involve distorted thinking, such as "Life isn't fair," or "I can't stand it." In truth, life *isn't* fair and you can stand anything except death, even if you don't happen to like it.

A Conversation with Myself

So, there I was, totally discouraged and frustrated. The principal of the school is a real controlling jerk, and everyone hates him. Every time I'd try to introduce some new idea, he'd shoot it down right away, never even give it a chance. The other teachers were really interested, but they were so afraid of the guy that they had to pretend they didn't care. I was ready to just give up, since I was just wasting my time. But then I had this conversation with myself—well, really it started out with someone over lunch and then continued long into the night when I was tossing and turning in bed, unable to sleep. I reminded myself that things don't change overnight, or certainly according to my time schedule. Things have been like this for eons, so who the hell am I to think I can just show up and that this will all be so easy? I'm blaming the principal—okay, he is pretty rigid—but he's just being protective. I've got to take a deep breath and recognize that this was never supposed to be easy, and I've set myself up for major disappointment by expecting that things would go according to my plan.

Once you can recognize these kinds of irrational thinking, as they take place inside your head or in your speech, then you are in a position to challenge them by asking yourself (or those you are helping) several pointed questions:

1. Where is the evidence that this is true?
2. Who says that life is fair?
3. How am I exaggerating or distorting this situation, blowing it out of proportion?
4. How is what I am doing getting in the way of what I really want?
5. What am I telling myself about this that is making things much worse?
6. How am I making myself upset over this situation that I can't control?

This is just the briefest sampling of relationship skills that prove useful to you during helping encounters, whether with individuals, families, or groups. The overriding principle is that you develop both interpersonal and cultural competence. This means developing awareness and understanding of the environmental and social context of your setting and then operating within it in such a way that you demonstrate respect, compassion, and caring. It is not enough that you put these skills into action unless your behavior is perceived by others as you intended. The only way you can find this out for sure is by collecting honest feedback from those you are helping. This, in itself, is a challenging task if such a question is considered rude and inappropriate.

We have mentioned repeatedly the ways that applying your skills in service to others can be incredibly transformative for you. In the next chapter, we look more deeply at the ways that travel experiences (loosely defined to include any cultural immersion) can provide you with powerful growth and learning that could not be obtained any other way.

CHAPTER 11

Travel That Can Change Your Life

Those who thrive on serving others in some capacity are also good at taking care of themselves. They attempt to model in their own lives the same values and priorities that they advocate for others. This includes taking constructive risks, promoting their own growth and development, working toward higher levels of functioning, and various forms of self-nurturance.

This book is not only about changing the world but also about changing yourself. There will be times when you are feeling depleted, exhausted, dispirited, even burned out, and it is crucial that you find ways to replenish your energy and push yourself to grow in new and exciting ways. Counseling, job changes, and further education are all reasonable options. But for someone committed to social justice and global human rights, one of the best ways to promote further growth is through your own travel experiences. We are not talking about traveling as a tourist, but rather as someone on a quest for further enlightenment. This enlightenment quest does not necessarily mean a trip to Tibet, Mt. Fuji, or the Kalahari Desert, but can involve a structured adventure that is designed to shake things up in your life a bit.

The word travel is derived from the old French, *travail*, meaning to labor, to sweat, to toil, to work hard at some activity. It implies, by definition, a challenging path filled with obstacles and a certain amount of anguish.

EFFECTS OF VOLUNTEER TRAVEL

In this chapter, we review the ways that a certain kind of *meaningful travel*, sometimes referred to as *voluntourism*, can inspire you in ways that augment

The best views are often obtained by climbing to the highest point, which requires considerable effort, discomfort, and pain. There is a direct relationship between how hard you push yourself and how much you will learn and grow as a result. The advantage of spending time in unfamiliar places and cultures is that you have greater opportunities to see, hear, feel, and sense things that might otherwise remain inaccessible.

whatever you learn in the classroom or through life experiences within your usual domain (Brown & Lehto, 2005). Such experiences include deeper emotional and spiritual elements that can last a lifetime (Wilson & Harris, 2006). The focus of our discussion is thus concentrated on how serving others changes *you* in the process. We specifically examine how, if you were inclined to do so, you could structure trips in such a way as to become life-changing.

When celebrities like Angelina Jolie, Brad Pitt, Oprah Winfrey, and Bono become involved in international charitable work, they are not only doing so to spread their vast wealth and influence, but also to create more meaning out of lives that are often dominated by the superficial aspects of the entertainment industry. So too do most of us get caught up in the mundane details of daily life, striving for success, fueling ambition, shopping, vying for more control. That is why it is so important to gain a greater global perspective, to get outside our normal lives, in order to better appreciate what it is that we have—and what we can offer to others.

So These Guys Walked into the Bar . . .

I love cars. I'm a total car guy. I go to the conventions, get all the fixings for my own ride. I love it. I'm almost 33, still work as a bartender, and to be honest I'm feeling like things haven't progressed for me that much since college. I've had a lot of fun, that is definitely for sure, but all those things I used to do for fun aren't as exciting anymore. Things are getting more and more dull, and to be honest, being a bartender just isn't as cool as it was when I was 26. I need a change, but I don't know where to go, or what I what to change. I've always felt like I need to have everything figured out before I take the next step. The other day these guys were in town visiting the local church to talk about some schools they were building down in El Salvador. First of all, I don't know what they were doing in a bar if they were in town to speak at a church, but whatever. They seemed like cool guys. I ran my life situation by them and we had a long, long bar-style chat, and these guys actually invited me to come on their next mission to South America. Man, I was into it. It hit me on a very powerful gut level. I felt excitement inside of me like I haven't felt forever—I think I'm going to do it. Lord knows I need to get out of this place.

There is actually scant literature on the subject of how travel changes people in profound ways, with the exception of some classic travel memoirs (see Cahill, 1996; Rapoport & Castenera, 1994; and Theroux, 1992 as examples). While there has been some attention to the ways that adventure-based activities can be personally growth-producing (Asher, Huffaker, & McNally, 1994; Gillis & Simpson, 1991) very few attempts have been made to design trips specifically for this purpose (Kottler, 1997). Notable exceptions include programs such as Outward Bound (www.outwardbound.com), Project Adventure (www.pa.org), Roadtrip Nation (www.roadtripnation.com), and Semester at Sea (www.semesteratsea.com), which design adventure-based trips that teach leadership skills, expand awareness of oneself and the world, and boost confidence. Many of these programs have elements

Students who volunteer on service learning projects, especially those who work as part of a team, develop greater social skills and self-confidence that prove useful throughout life. They also develop invaluable real-life experiences that make their academic studies come alive.

in common with what occurs during independent transformative sojourns. First of all, they often lead to self-empowerment and self-confidence; secondly, they promote a greater sense of connectedness to others (Wilson & Harris, 2006).

Students who volunteer on service learning projects while in school tend to develop greater optimism and hope in other aspects of their lives, including their academic performance (Ryder, 2006). In one study of students who volunteered abroad, participants consistently reported a number of positive changes. Most notably, they felt the experience enhanced their self-confidence and helped them to appreciate better the complexity of the world and their relationships, leading to greater maturity and a sense of personal identity (Schmidt, 2000). In other words, they returned more seasoned and wise about the world in ways they could never learn in the classroom or on campus. In another study of people who volunteered to work in community projects while traveling abroad in their youth, there was a strong theme of spiritual transcendence that took place for them, an experience that lasted throughout their lifetimes (Zahra, 2006).

Volunteer travel has sometimes been characterized as "overpriced guilt trips with an impact as fleeting as the feel-good factor" (Fitzpatrick, 2007, p. 49). People pay a little extra to visit some village, teach in a school for a week, build a house or road, and then can relax on the beach with an easier conscience. Similarly, students might devote one semester to a service learning project less out of altruistic motives than to fortify their resumes and build a portfolio for graduate school or the corporate world.

Combining volunteer service with a trip abroad is also one of the hottest new kinds of tourism, and travel agents are ramping up to meet the demand. People go on holidays in the first place not just for relaxation but for rejuvenation. While sitting on the beach or poolside does qualify in some ways, more and more people are looking for something more active that promotes self-development and self-discovery. Ironically, one of the most proven ways to facilitate this process is not through self-indulgence but through service to others (Coghlan, 2006). A half million young people have volunteered for AmeriCorp since its inception in 1994; even more have worked for the Peace Corp around the world.

Dreaming about Travel

I do have one big dream that I haven't really spoken about for a while. When I was a kid, I used to love watching Jacques Cousteau as he traveled the world on his boat. I always wanted to be an adventurer like that, but I'm from Mississippi, and no one around here does that kind of stuff. Most people have never even been to Atlanta before! Television seems like our only way out, at least I know it is for me. Discovery Channel is my favorite channel. I watch the National Geographic Channel as well. I always get those junk-mail messages from travel companies saying "Go to South America from $300," which I can afford, so why am I not going? What's keeping me back? I honestly don't know. My family always gives me a hard time about my dreams, but it's not like they've chained me to the bed or anything. I've got to figure this out, and I'm getting the feeling more and more like it's now or never. And I don't want to be one of those people who hasn't even been to Atlanta before.

CLARIFYING AN AGENDA

Louellen was a busy, overworked student who was also juggling responsibilities as a part-time worker, as a daughter to ailing parents, and as the social organizer for her family and friends. Whereas her boyfriend, Mark, felt the need to continuously push the limits of adventure-oriented activities from mountain biking to rock climbing, Louellen felt she had altogether too much excitement in her life—what she longed for was greater peace. Her sleep was often disrupted with head-spinning plans about what she might do to increase her efficiency at work, improve her grades, or care for her parents as their health continued to deteriorate. She was not eating properly nor taking care of herself nearly as well as she was ministering to the needs of her family and friends.

When it came time for Louellen and Mark to plan for an upcoming summer break, they realized how different their agendas were. Mark wanted to head south to Mexico, where they might partake in a staggering assortment of activities available. They could go surfing, take scuba lessons, or go parasailing or river rafting, then at night they could hang out in local bars and drink tequila. "Doesn't that sound great?" Mark asked her as he showed her the colorful web site, his eyes alight with the unlimited possibilities.

Louellen, however, had a different sort of holiday in mind, one that might help her regain control over a life that felt as if it was spinning chaotically wherever forces pulled her. The prospect of being in an environment where people expected her to stay constantly in motion would hardly be a welcome break. She would just be trading one set of commitments for another.

When Mark asked her what she would most enjoy, Louellen was surprised to hear herself blurt out that she'd love to be locked in a monastery. There would be time to rest and think. No distractions of television, telephones, video games, and her computer. Nobody else to care for. She would be able just to think about her life and where she was headed. She could sort out what was really most important to her among the daily chores that kept her so busy she had no time for reflection.

"So, why don't you go to a monastery then, if that's what you really want?" Mark seemed serious. "Hey, I'll go with some friends to Mexico instead, give you some time on your own. You find a mountaintop to sit on where you can eat brown rice, mutter 'ohmmmm' to yourself, or whatever you do at a monastery."

Louellen did exactly that. Rather than traveling halfway around the world to Tibet, she found a retreat center just outside the city where she lived. She spent a week doing nothing but sleeping and eating simple meals whenever she felt like it. Without a watch or any schedule to follow, she did whatever she liked. She went for long walks. She meditated. And for a whole week she neither heard nor spoke a single word.

Under such circumstances, perhaps you're not the least surprised to find that Louellen returned from her "travels" a bit different than before she left. She felt refreshed and invigorated. She felt resolved to make some changes in her life that might continue the new spirit that had been awakened.

Louellen's boyfriend, Mark? Oh, he had a great time. Played in the surf. Partied day and night. But it wasn't change he was after.

ACTING OUT OF CHARACTER

Whereas Louellen's story is one in which she immersed herself totally in a different environment that allowed her to think, feel, and react in novel ways, such a total shift is rarely necessary. The simple act of leaving home is sometimes enough for many people to act out of their usual roles.

Madeleine, for example, is ordinarily very eager to please. She has played the roles of adoring daughter, dutiful wife, doting mother, and loyal employee all her life. If you asked people who know Madeleine best what she is like, you would hear the word "sweet" mentioned again and again. Indeed she *is* sweet in the best sense of the word, essentially kind and considerate. Still, if there is one problem that has plagued her throughout her life, it has been that she has taken such good care of others, she sometimes neglects herself. As such, she is reluctant to assert herself and rarely participates in conflict.

Perhaps that is why her husband, Wayne, was so shocked by what he witnessed during their vacation. They had just arrived at the airport of their destination, weary and irritable. After claiming their luggage, they walked outside to find a taxi where an airport guard pointed to a spot they should stand. As they proceeded to the appointed station, they overheard the guard yelling at them to stand somewhere else; apparently they had at first misunderstood him. Just as they adjusted their position, they once again heard the man yelling at them.

Madeleine had had quite enough. She calmly walked up to him, and in a voice that neither she nor her husband had ever heard before, she told him she thought he was really rude and there was no call to scream at people. If this was how people in his city treated newcomers, it was a wonder anyone ever came back.

The guard looked at her as though she were insect he was debating whether to squash. "Look, lady, are you deaf or something? Just get out of the way and let me do my job."

"You, sir, are not a very nice person, nor are you particularly helpful." With that, Madeleine, turned and strode away with a determination her husband had never seen before.

Whatever made her act so out of character? How is it that a woman could spend her life so willing to please others, to avoid conflict at all costs, and then all of a sudden erupt into an assertive spokesperson for the traveling downtrodden?

Actually, several factors were at work. Madeleine was tired and vulnerable, her nerves stretched tight. Secondly, her husband had not been feeling well. Whereas normally he would take care of everything, his relative docility throughout the journey stimulated Madeleine to take a more active role. Most of all, however, it was being away from her usual environment, the normal cues and obligations, the people and schedules that ruled her life, that permitted her the freedom to be someone different. Those same possibilities are open to you.

CREATING A TRANSFORMATIVE TRIP

Both Louellen and Madeleine were changed significantly as a result of their travel experiences. Of course, not everyone is interested in such dramatic changes in their lives. But for those who are motivated to move in new directions, psychotherapy isn't always the best solution. As a therapist and trainer of other therapists, Jeffrey admits that he has been impatient with how long change often takes. If someone *really* wanted to change his or her life, and do it quickly, creating a transformative trip might just be the answer.

Reluctance to Travel Abroad

I will never forget watching those airplanes fly into the World Trade Center when I was a kid. It was shocking! Ever since then, it's seemed like the world is such a dangerous, scary place. Why would I ever want to put myself in a situation where I could be get killed or something? Now I'm a freshman in college, and I would like to try and make a difference in the world, but it seems like all the places you have to go to are really dangerous, and it would be stupid to go out there. America feels so much safer it makes me just want to mostly travel around here. Maybe if the world ever calms down, and terrorism isn't as bad any more, I'll start thinking about going to other countries.

Based on research conducted on this subject over a period of years (Gebhard, Marriner, & Gordon, 2003; Kottler, 1997; Kottler & Montgomery, 2000; Marriner, McAllister, Gebhard, & Bollinger, 2005) we offer the following tips for creating your own transformative adventures.

Make a List of What You Want to Do, Then . . . Throw It Away

Yes, you heard us correctly. It is not where you go that matters, or even for how long; the key is which opportunities you take advantage of along the way. If you take the time to interview people about the travels that have had the most enduring impact on their lives (as we have done), consistently they will tell stories of serendipitous encounters. In spite of their best laid plans and most meticulous itineraries, it is not museums, tour buses, and sanctioned tourist sites that are most likely to inspire you. We are not saying that visits to rich cultural locales are not valuable and educational; rather we are suggesting that that you get off the beaten path.

Think about a time in your life when you felt a dramatic impact from some sort of trip or travel experience. This event or process was so influential that it forever altered the way you see yourself, and the rest of the world. Almost everyone has a story to tell, and interestingly, most of these experiences were not altogether pleasant at the time. In fact, it appears that the most constructive life-altering trips were those that involved some sort of awful, traumatic, or uncomfortable events that forced the person to develop new resources, increase confidence, and to solve problems in new ways. Oh, the stories afterwards may sound very amusing and quite fun, but actually they were not nearly as enjoyable at the time. Quite often, they involved being hopelessly lost, miserable, or frightened. In other words, there was some type of emotional activation that made the person ripe for altered perceptions.

The implication of this premise is interesting, because it means that the best things that happen on trips are those events that were unplanned, unanticipated, and often involved difficult challenges to be overcome. As long as people stay on tour buses, stay in comfortable hotels, eat familiar foods, and stick with guides and planned itineraries, they may have a lovely time, but they will probably not experience personal transformation. They will return rested and relaxed, but the effects will not often last very long. But once people stray from what is predictable, force themselves to take constructive risks, embrace unstructured time, or allow themselves to get lost, wonderful things can happen—if the person is not seriously traumatized and has the opportunity to process the experience in a systematic way.

GET LOST

As we mentioned, the most enduring memories often occur as a result of unanticipated and unforeseen experiences. It is when things go wrong, when you encounter the unexpected, that you are most likely to be changed. When your luggage is lost, when you miss a flight or train, when you wander off course, when you become disoriented—then the real action begins. "The glory of travel," writes adventurer Pico Iyer, "is that one always—always—gets lost. A trip is measured, really, only by how far we stop off the expected path, stumble into things we never wanted to see, fall between the cracks and the words on the schedule-sheet, in effect, and tumble into mystery" (Curwen, 2007, p. L5).

Our favorite story illustrating this premise involves a young woman, Claire, who was traveling in Europe with her husband. They had a fairly codependent relationship, meaning that Claire liked to be taken care of and that her husband, Matt, liked to be in control. For Claire, this meant that she enjoyed not worrying about where they were going in life, or on this trip, but at the expense of surrendering a lot of freedom and independence. Since Matt was good at arranging things and taking care of all the innumerable details involved in their European sojourn, Claire told herself she didn't mind their negotiated division of labor.

Claire and Matt were traveling by train across the continent, on their way to Italy, or Switzerland—Claire couldn't remember what was next. They were in a comfortable sleeping berth and Claire had been easily lulled to sleep by the rocking motions of the train. She awakened in the middle of the night, having to go to the bathroom, or the WC as the facility was clearly marked on the door.

Claire climbed down from her bunk, noticed Matt was soundly sleeping, and so decided to venture out on her own. She walked to the end of the car to find the door to the toilet locked; someone was inside. She waited for a minute, then another, but since she had to go very badly she decided to go on to the toilet in the next car. This one had a sign on the door, in four different languages, all proclaiming that the facility was out of order. Now what was she going to do? She had to go very, very badly and didn't think she could wait much longer.

It was at that point that she realized the train was no longer moving. She looked out the window to find that sometime in the middle of the night the train had boarded some kind of ship or ferry. The train was on a boat? Now, she remembered: they were crossing a lake, Lake Lugano or something like that, that separated two countries. Surely this boat or ship or whatever it was had a bathroom she could use.

Strolling among the rows of cars that were parked on board, Claire eventually found a stairway going up to the next floor. Since she was wearing only her nightgown, not having considered she needed anything else to walk to the toilet at the end of the hall, she was feeling more than a little self-conscious about her appearance. She poked her head out the stairway door, to find a lot of people walking around, so she ducked back inside and headed up another floor, all the while trying to concentrate on not peeing on herself. Finally, in what seemed like forever, she located a toilet and relieved herself. See, that wasn't so bad, was it?

Feeling proud of her little exploration, she tried to retrace her steps back to the train, but the storage area was so cavernous that it took her quite a while to cover the territory. She spent 20 fruitless minutes searching for the train.

Where could it be? It was a huge, long line of cars attached to a monstrous engine. Hard to lose a train.

For the second time that evening, she noticed that she could feel no movement. With horror, she discovered that during her absence, the ship had docked at the port and the train had left. Without her!

Claire burst into tears as she realized that she was now totally alone and totally helpless. She was standing in her nightgown and slippers. In a foreign country. She didn't even know *which* country she was in. She couldn't speak the language. She had no passport. No money. No phone. No way to communicate with anyone. And no husband around to tell her what to do.

Claire wandered out of the ship onto the pier and did the only thing she could think of to do—she sat down on the curb and cried. After several minutes of despair, she decided this wasn't doing much good. Her sisters had warned her that some day her dependence on Matt would leave her stuck. She had even started therapy once to work on this issue, but dropped out when she realized that she *liked* Matt taking care of her. What was the harm if they both liked the arrangement?

Walking around the shipyard, Claire noticed a train sitting idle at the station. She was cold and shivering in her nightgown, utterly terrified by her predicament. With no other choice, she boarded the train, hoping for a little warmth and the company of some other people, even if she couldn't communicate with them. What would she do when the conductor came to ask for her ticket and her passport? Would they put her in jail or just kick her off the train?

Such were her thoughts when the train stopped several minutes later at the next station. With increasing desperation, Claire search for an option. Should she get off the train or keep riding as long as she could—wherever the train was going? She didn't even know where Matt was headed, since he was in charge of their itinerary. How stupid could she be? Here she was in some strange, godforsaken place with no idea of how to take care of herself. She had no resources. No way to communicate. All she had was this stupid nightgown. And now people were looking at her strangely.

Looking out the window, she noticed another train sitting across the tracks. But this wasn't just any train—this was *her* train—she was sure of it. She recognized the distinctive colors of the cars. With little thought, she bolted her current sanctuary, ran across the tracks like a madwoman, and jumped aboard the train just before it began moving again. Out of breath, Claire made her way through the cars until she once again relocated her berth. Matt was still sleeping, never aware she'd even been gone. The bastard.

As she climbed back into her bunk, shivering with cold and fear, she realized that the anger she felt towards Matt was really best directed toward herself. She was the one who had allowed herself to become so helpless and dependent that she barely had an idea where she was going, much less how to take care of herself if things went astray. She had become lost on this trip just as she had in her own life back home.

Claire vowed that in the morning, when Matt woke up, they had some renegotiation to do in their relationship. As much as she appreciated and valued her husband's love and devotion, it was no longer acceptable to her that she surrender all decisions. She could enjoy a loving relationship with her husband and yet do so without totally losing herself.

Resolutions such as this are not uncommon after a traumatic experience. People often make such declarations in the throes of relief after finding safety. But in this case, Claire did follow through on her commitment. Many years later, when she related this story of transformative travel, she described all the work she had done since then. She now presented herself as a remarkably resourceful, successful, and confident woman. And she still enjoyed a close, intimate relationship with Matt—who had been required to make a number of adjustments in his own life to accommodate the new, independent Claire.

It took getting lost—completely and utterly lost—for Claire to experience significant growth. Her sisters' advice, her work in therapy, and her own inner yearnings had not been enough without this definitive moment in her life. This is the sort of epiphany that can be possible during travels but cannot happen within our normal states of consciousness.

CREATE A MINDSET FOR CHANGE

You are much more likely to be transformed by an experience if that is what you expect and plan for. While dramatic changes can take place without planning—and often do—you can significantly increase the probability of such an impact by adopting a particular mindset. Any time you do your homework and educate yourself about an upcoming event, the more the subtleties and depth of the experience will be revealed to you. Likewise, certain attitudes can predispose you to be influenced in ways that might not otherwise occur.

This means adopting an attitude of patience and forbearance, prepared to deal with the inevitable delays, disappointments, and annoyances. Getting unduly upset and angry about things that are outside your control (e.g., flight cancellations, smallpox epidemics, lost luggage, newly erupted civil wars, intestinal distress, blizzards, long lines, bureaucratic snafus, blind alleys, miscommunications, turbulence) in the air or on the ground only make irritations become major sources of perceived disaster. "At the very least," one writer comments about the spoiled, petulant nature that many travelers seem to have adopted, "anger is the patina of a good travel story. The greatest inconvenience, the greatest pique, elevates the adventure (especially back home), and once we understand that, we can see that humility is the most important lesson any trip can impart" (Curwin, 2007, p. L5). Humility indeed.

CLARIFY YOUR GOALS

Part of your mindset in undertaking service-oriented travel is to clarify your motives for doing so. There are a number of reasons why people travel in the first place, many of which are listed below (Brown & Lehto, 2005):

- *Escape from the routine*. Much of daily life is predictable, repetitive, even boring at times when things are overstructured. Travel gives people the opportunity to let go of their patterns.
- *Time out for reflection*. Most people are so busy that they rarely have time to consider where they have been, where they are now, and where they are going next. The hectic pace of life, plus all the diversions and distractions provided by media, make it difficult to spend time thinking about plans and dreams for the future.
- *Relaxation*. Vacations are designed to "vacate" your mind so you can relax, rejuvenate, and replenish your energy before jumping back into the chaos of life.
- *Escape into pleasure*. Travel can be completely hedonistic in nature; some people seek as much pleasure as they can find. Drinking, drugs, sex, massages, anything that helps one to "let go" may be the major priority.

- *Social interaction*. People travel to meet people and make new friends or find a sense of community (such as in group tours).
- *Adventure*. Physical challenges, such as hiking, mountain climbing, scuba diving, or cycling, give participants ways to test themselves or engage in strenuous physical activities. Risk taking may be part of the experience as well, especially those who hunger for greater stimulation.
- *Prestige*. People sometimes travel as a form of consumption. People attain status in all kinds of ways—often with material possessions, such as cars, homes, watches, clothes, but also by taking certain trips that present a particular image.
- *Education*. Learning can be a significant part of travel for people, especially those interested in culture, history, architecture, and art.
- *Service*. People can make a point to travel somewhere to do something useful for others. Only in the last few decades has this entry been added to the list.

Regardless of the reason you *think* you are traveling—for research, class credit, internship, adventure, semester abroad, language acquisition, service learning, or simply leisure—it is important to remain open to whatever the experience brings you. As long as you remain focused on your self-declared goal, you may close yourself off to other opportunities that might arise.

INSULATE YOURSELF FROM THE USUAL INFLUENCES THAT RULE YOUR LIFE

The best way we know to promote significant learning and growth is for you to immerse yourself in a novel environment, one that is likely to challenge you to solve problems in new ways. Part of the beauty of travel is getting far away from your comfort zone. It can be an uncomfortable process, because human nature is to cling to safety and comfort as a mechanism for survival. But if real challenge and growth is to occur, the environment you're engaged in has to feel and be foreign. It's kind of like lifting weights. The only way to increase muscle mass is to first break your muscle fiber down, to actually tear those fibers, which then causes them to grow back even stronger. You still need a healthy environment so that the healing process can be nurtured, but at the end of that process, there is more strength than there would have been before the muscle was put under that stress.

When Ryan traveled to Uganda, he had no idea what to expect. An experienced traveler who had just come off an extended trip across America, he knew that he needed something different to really get his attention. Even though he knew he was putting himself in an uncomfortable third-world environment, he still had no idea how hard it would be.

While in Uganda, he visited international aid-workers, specifically medical doctors on the front lines of AIDS and starvation, professionals who were dedicating their lives to help the people of Africa. Ryan had an inkling of an idea that he might want to go into medicine someday and use his skills to help impoverished people, but it was always something that he felt deep below the surface, on a level where he could barely even admit it to himself.

In Uganda, Ryan encountered the most dramatic poverty he could have ever imagined. People were actually dying on the streets, and he was helpless to do anything about it. He saw violent crime on horrific levels. He felt that his own safety was constantly in jeopardy, especially when flying on rickety planes to remote regions; more than once he was certain they were going to crash.

When Ryan got home from his trip, the feelings he'd had about becoming a doctor in the developing world began to show themselves. He began to verbally share with friends and family that he wanted to become a doctor, and someday go back to Africa with those skills to make a difference. He had seen firsthand the run-down clinics and depressed shanty towns and he'd learned that he could handle it. It was shocking at first, but the more time he spent in Uganda, the more his own inner strength and character came out. And once this emerged, he saw himself, and his future, in a much clearer light. His passion for making a difference in the world was no longer buried by apprehension and fear. He had faced those uncomfortable environments, knew he could handle them, and now would not let that uncertainty hold him back.

EMBRACE EMOTIONAL AROUSAL

Fear, apprehension, anxiety, uncertainty, and discomfort are the precise emotions that help you hold on to experiences and remember them throughout your lifetime. During the times when you are feeling upset and wishing that things could be more predictable and comfortable, remind yourself that is when the real growth and action are taking place. Of course, Ryan tried that as his plane was nose-diving or a menacing guy with a machete was approaching him on the street—"If this doesn't kill me, it will make me stronger"—but it didn't seem to offer much comfort. It was only after he was back home that he appreciated that the most emotional experiences, related to fear, joy, exhilaration, and despair, were actually the ones that had the most powerful effects.

Here's another example. The plan was to spend two days in a remote mountain hut in Iceland, located on the largest glacier in this part of the world. I (Jeffrey) was working on a photographic book about winter in Iceland and needed to capture images of this spectacular region of high mountain peaks, smoky volcanoes, and thermal lakes with floating icebergs. If things had gone as planned, I would have done my job and moved on with my life. Like most tourists, I would have had the photos to remind myself of my adventure, but the memories would have quickly faded.

My two partners and I were beset by one disaster after another. First, the moment after we arrived, the weather turned treacherous, making visibility impossible. It snowed so much and the wind howled so hard that we couldn't even leave the tiny hut. To stay warm, we walked around in circles much of the day and took turns leading aerobic classes to keep ourselves from freezing to death. What little food we had froze solid. We tried to call for help, but the radio did not work properly, so we were stranded. Day after day we waited for rescue, watching our supplies of food and fuel grow perilously short. We got acute cabin fever and started going for walks and ski expeditions in the blizzard outside. When the weather finally broke, nobody came to get us, even though it was three days beyond our scheduled pick-up.

Since I spent about 12 hours a day in my sleeping bag trying to stay warm, it was not until relatively late that I looked outside to see a glorious day outside—bright sun, two feet of fresh snow, and the most spectacular mountain scenery you could imagine. Even though we were still abandoned, still stuck in this isolated, dangerous place, with no way to get out, I still had one of the most amazing days of my life (maybe because I imagined it as one of my last).

By the time the rescue team came to pull us out, we had all given up hope. We were reduced to preparing a dinner of peanut butter on raw pasta. We were using snowballs instead of toilet paper. Truth be told, we were despondent. I can't recall ever feeling so miserable.

Looking back on the experience, I would not trade it for anything. I kept a journal throughout the ordeal, writing down every thought, feeling, and conversation that took place between us. I made some new resolutions about my life, which I am still in the process of implementing. The world looks different to me now, as does my life. It would have taken me years of therapy to get to the same point. Most of the growth took place precisely because I felt so emotionally overwrought. One lesson learned: when you are most aroused, most emotional, most stimulated, then you have the greatest potential to make lifelong changes that will endure.

Search Out Novel Environments

In a study of 39 astronauts and cosmonauts who had been on extended spaceflights (just about the most novel environment one can imagine), every one of them reported strong personal changes that took place in their attitudes and behavior after they returned to Earth. It didn't matter how long they had been in space, how many missions they had been on previously, or any demographic features such as their age, gender, or profession—all of them experienced meaningful and permanent transformations from their space travel (Ihle, Ritsher, & Kanas, 2006).

Among students who went on a more terrestrial voyage—a "Semester at Sea"—interviews indicated that the vast majority continued to experience tremendous growth even decades after the trip ended. This was especially the case with regard to the meaning they found in their lives and work (Dukes, 2006). That is one reason why educational institutions encourage students to spend a semester abroad or to sign up for service learning.

Although it isn't necessary to leave home in order to promote dramatic changes, it sure helps to do so. The more unusual the environment, at least based on your own experience, the more likely that you are going to be strongly impacted by novel stimuli. It means going to places (figuratively and literally) that you have not visited before.

I (Jeffrey) spent a week living in a remote, tiny hunting village in East Greenland, just hanging out with the people, visiting the school, playing with the children, riding dogsleds to look for seals or polar bears. Truth be told, it was an extremely uncomfortable week—defecating in buckets, trying to stay warm, struggling to make sense of communications with people when we did not share a common language. If only a plane came more than once a week, I would have left early a dozen different times. But I was forced to stay, forced to deal with what I faced, and much of the time I didn't much enjoy it. It was only after I returned and had time to reflect on what happened that I realized how much I had learned about myself.

EXPERIMENT WITH NEW WAYS OF BEING

Travel is about being in motion, about spontaneity and breaking routines, about taking constructive risks. Since nobody knows you when you are on the road, you can reinvent yourself. In your usual environment, your parents, friends, siblings, classmates, and coworkers all have specific expectations of how you are to act, based on ways you have behaved previously. Many people report that when they try to make changes in their lives, other people won't let them. What they really mean is that it is difficult to change routines and patterns when we navigate through the same environment.

When you're on the road, however, especially when you are alone, you have the opportunity to reinvent yourself, since nobody knows what the "real" you is supposed to be like. If you are ordinarily shy, you can be assertive; if you are prone to hanging back, you can initiate—and the people around don't know that this isn't the way you usually act.

Travel also presents you with a set of challenges in which your usual ways of solving problems may not work very well. There are often different names and terms to describe things in various parts of the world. And certainly there are foreign customs in new lands.

PLAN FOR RE-ENTRY

The sad truth is that the effects of travel (or any change effort like dieting, self-help programs, workshops, and so on) don't last long. You must build changes into your daily life. It helps to make public commitments of what you intend to do differently. This means telling anyone and everyone you know—or at least those who care enough to listen—about what you intend to do differently in the future. It is harder to make excuses, procrastinate, and avoid following through when you have gone "on record."

If you have been keeping a journal about the journey, you have one vehicle by which to process experiences systematically. It is not enough to have an amazing travel adventure or transformative experience unless you make the effort to make sense of the experience, to create personal meaning, to generalize from one situation to others.

Okay, so you have had a memorable trip. You have learned a lot and had a magnificent time. You are positively glowing from the encounter. You say that this changed your life. Now prove it! Let's see what you can do to apply what you learned to so many areas of your life that have characteristically given you trouble.

The two most important questions to address are:

1. So what?
2. What now?

We think of travel as being separate from our normal lives, a respite, a moratorium, a time out that eventually ends once we return home. Yet each of us is traveling every moment of our lives, whether we define it as a vacation or not. Wherever you are, whomever you are with, whatever the circumstances, travel is a state of mind in which you attend to your movements through space, and time.

You need not be in Tahiti or Madagascar to be transformed by your journey. Taking a trip, even an adventurous, unstructured one, is no guarantee that you will grow significantly and permanently as a result. Just getting out of bed in the morning in a particular way, facing the day with a spirit of adventure, encountering people with openness and flexibility, pushing yourself to do things differently, is what creates personal growth.

While it is often easier to do this during a trip, away from usual influences and restrictions, these changes can take place anywhere you choose to make them happen. In fact, if travel teaches you one important lesson, it is that life is too sweet and short to limit your freedom to mere vacations. Travel is not really an escape from normal life, nor is it an insulated reality; rather, it acts as a reminder of what is possible for you to experience every waking moment of your life. When you seize this possibility, you will never be the same again.

In the stories included in this section of the book, we provide an incredibly broad spectrum of possibilities in terms of the ways that people just like you become involved in projects designed to promote global human rights and social justice issues. We hope they inspire you to think about ways that you might become more actively involved in your own community or anywhere else that calls to you.

CHAPTER 12

International Jetsetters

This chapter is the first of several that profile stories and insights from people who are actually out in the field, taking action and changing lives all over the world. What have they learned from their experiences? How did they figure out which path was the right one for them? And what advice do they have for others who also want to make a difference in the world?

What the stories in this chapter have in common is an international focus. Most of the organizational founders were exposed to travel during their college years, experiences that haunted and inspired them in certain ways. They had developed a love for adventure and an appreciation for the people they met along the way. They were moved by the plight of those who are subjected to life-threatening challenges. They had grown up, just like the rest of us, watching video footage on the news of starving children in Africa, or destitute street-people in India, Brazil, Indonesia, or the Middle East, and decided they just had to do something. They couldn't be observers any longer; they had to take some kind of action.

You will not have heard of most of these people. With few exceptions, they don't make their way into the media, nor are they featured on talk shows or magazine covers. Yet they are working across the globe in some of the most inhospitable places on Earth, trying to help local communities turn their lives around. Contained within these stories are not only case studies of what can be done to advocate on behalf of human rights and social justice issues, but also the inspiration for you to become involved in ways to make the best use of your talents and interests.

Believe You Can Make a Difference:
Ariane Kirtley, Founder of Amman Imman

The first step in doing something worthwhile is believing that it is within your capacity to do so. Ariane Kirtley, founder of Amman Imman — Water is Life — admits that the idea that any of us can really make much of a difference might seem preposterous when the scope and magnitude of human problems seem so overwhelming. Yet she believes that this is not only possible but highly likely, if you trust yourself and persist in your efforts. If you fail the first time, or don't meet your expectations, then just change the goals to those within reach. This idea of "thinking small" is a theme we will revisit again and again. It is from such modest efforts that sometimes very large effects result.

"I was always taught that if I have a dream or a vision, to go for it," Ariane explained. "My parents always encouraged me to do that and never take a traditional path. So if you see something, or are passionate about something, even if everyone tells you it is impossible, trust your instincts, and believe that you can make a difference. Even if no one else out there wants to make a difference or even pay attention to what the issue really is, go for it, run for it, because you only have one life. And you have to make the most of the life that you have."

Ariane attributes this altruistic drive to her parents, but it is possible to develop such a passion at any stage in life, especially from instructors and mentors in college, where your main goal is to expand your interests and skills. All it takes is an openness to new ideas and a willingness to try some things you've never done before.

Ariane's parents were photographers for *National Geographic*, so her childhood was spent traveling the globe. From the time she was six months old, she was moving through Africa, living in Algeria, Gambia, Senegal, Mali, the Ivory Coast, and Niger. "We got to live in the bush, so I really grew up seeing how these people lived. I always looked to the people in these villages as my family, so when I went to university, I always knew I would go back to Africa and do something for them."

Ariane studied anthropology in college and later earned a master's degree in public health. During the summer of 2003, she returned to Niger in West Africa to intern for CARE International on a hygiene and sanitation program in

Ariane Kirtley, founder of Amman Imman, an organization that helps provide clean water for communities that are literally dying of thirst.

the rural areas of the Konni district. It was during that student internship that she first became aware of what would become her life's mission. She visited the Azawak region, the poorest place in one of the poorest countries in the world, a place inhabited by a half-million people without regular access to water. She was stunned to learn that the people walk 30 miles each day, 15 miles each way, to obtain water from a reliable source! In addition, the people have no access to schools or health care. They live in an area that is so remote that few government agencies or organizations even know that they exist.

Even with a lifetime of experience spent traveling and living throughout Africa, Ariane had never seen anything quite as tragic as the plight of the Azawak region. The place was calling out to her. If she didn't do something for these people, nobody else would. "I couldn't believe that nobody was doing anything to help these people who were dying of thirst. All over Niger, people were receiving packages of rice and millet, but in this region people had no clue that aid was even being given to other parts of Niger."

During her studies, Arianne learned that half of the children in the area died before the age of five, the highest mortality rate in the world. Many of these children died of malnutrition, disease, and starvation, but a great number died simply because they had nothing to drink. It was all the more remarkable because it wasn't that they had no access to clean water, but to any water at all.

Once she discovered what was going on, Ariane naively believed that all she would have to do is to tell people what was going on and they'd do something. "CARE International tried to help. They sent a team up there to check out the situation, and were blown away by the poverty. But my proposal [to dig wells in the area] was denied, because international aid agencies don't want to work in such a remote and difficult area. Secondly, nomadic people are hard to work with, because they are constantly moving. And thirdly, most of the people in this region are minority ethnic groups that most people are not interested in helping."

This is the point in the story at which most people would give up. You found a dire situation. You saw a need that you could fill. You came home, knocked on doors, begged organizations for support, talked to people in power about what could be done, and all you got were rejections and discouragement. Your conscience clear that you had done all you could, you'd shrug and move on to something more practical and feasible, something that you could actually accomplish.

But for Ariane, the more excuses she heard, the more furious and determined she became to persist in her goals. "I thought these excuses were complete crap. First of all, it wasn't dangerous at all. People were extremely kind and generous to me everywhere I went. I never felt threatened. But most importantly, people were dying! I knew that something had to be done, and that if I wasn't going to do it, no one would."

One thing that was stressed repeatedly in Ariane's education was that one should never, *ever* try to do anything on your own, that you must work within existing organizations and infrastructure; anything else, is doomed to failure. But what do you do when nobody will help? She couldn't just walk away.

Ariane launched her own grassroots organization called Amman Imman (translated as "water is life"), which eventually became part of The Friendship

Caravan, an American organization dedicated to promoting multicultural understanding through educational programs and humanitarian outreach. Ariane figured she needed to raise a minimum of $250,000 to dig just two wells because the water was so far underground, estimated to be at least 1,000 feet. From her research, she learned that contractors would need to bring in oil drilling equipment to dig that far.

Because she grew up in a family of photographers, Ariane used her own talents to take photos of the people of Azawak to show in exhibitions; these turned out to become excellent fundraising forums. Other people jumped on board with the project, attracting donors and sponsors, organizing athletic events and walkathons. Much to her surprise, Ariane actually enjoyed the fundraising part of her plan. Now came the really hard part.

"I went back to Niger and did some research on what kind of infrastructure needed to be built, and dealt with government authorities—where the corruption and greed was unbelievable. You had to bribe people everywhere. I had to stay very morally solid and not pay bribes. Then we had problems internally with people we worked with who were not in it for the right reasons. There was a lot to deal with."

By her reference to the "right" reasons, Ariane is bringing attention to the reality that people volunteer for a variety of reasons that have nothing to do with helping people and everything to do with inflating their own egos and status within the community. People have hidden and ulterior motives that may not be visible until much later. This is one reason it is so crucial to work with those you really trust.

The physical challenges of working in 120-degree heat were also brutal for Ariane. "I had to remind myself that I was saving lives, and that I only have one life to live. I knew that I had to live my passion, live my dream, no matter what anyone else told me."

In 2007, Ariane and her team completed the first well, hopefully the first of many she will build in the future. "I saw my friends literally dying. I was afraid to go back and see who had died since I had been gone. These weren't just statistics—these were my friends! They had literally offered me their last bowl of water. I couldn't let them down. I made a promise to them I would come back with water, but I had no idea how difficult it would be to keep that vow. I know now that we've done something pretty amazing, saving people's lives."

TAKE THE NEXT STEP: ELIZABETH HAUSLER, BUILD CHANGE

She grew up in a small town in Illinois, but it's amazing to see how far Elizabeth Hausler has come building her own grassroots organization, which travels across the globe helping victims of earthquake devastation. Elizabeth's organization aims to greatly reduce deaths, injuries, and economic losses caused by housing collapses due to earthquakes in developing countries. The organization works with international agencies and local engineers, architects, builders, and homeowners to promote and build with low-cost, earthquake resistant construction methods that will continue to be used once they leave the village.

As with so many of our stories, Elizabeth's circuitous route hasn't been the result of perfect planning but rather a continuous process of trial and error that aligns her passions with unaddressed social issues. It is also interesting how her project eventually became an extension of her earliest training as the daughter of a building contractor, working as a brick mason during the summers between school. "I loved that work," Elizabeth recalls, "because I could actually see what I accomplished by the end of the day."

When Elizabeth went to college, she chose to build on what she learned working with her father by majoring in engineering. Once she graduated, she began working in a field that combined engineering and business with her interest in environmental sustainability. She became frustrated with the adversarial nature of relationships between engineering and environmental types, so she decided to give herself some time off to explore the world a bit, and she moved to a ski town in Colorado. "I know this wasn't exactly moving to India or anything, but it made sense at the time. It was just a matter of taking the first step."

While living in Steamboat Springs, Elizabeth met people from all over the world, expanding her horizons far beyond small-town life in the midwest. Her political and career interests changed as a result of these conversations, leading her to enroll in graduate school. About halfway through school, three life-changing things took place. First, she met a man who had started a company in Africa that helped people gain access to equipment that promoted development, such as irrigation pumps, hay balers, and oil seed presses. This opened her eyes to what engineers could do to help those who were most in need.

"The second thing was that a huge earthquake hit India in 2001 and killed more than 20,000 people. I was studying that kind of stuff at Berkeley, and when

Elizabeth Hausler is the founder of Build Change, an organization that helps people recover from catastrophic earthquakes in developing countries.

I looked at the collapsed buildings, I realized that they were not reinforced. That's when I realized that it wasn't the earthquake that killed the people—it was the buildings themselves. I figured there must be some kind of solution."

The final impetus for Elizabeth's transformation occurred on September 11, 2001, when she realized that she just had to do something more useful with her engineering skills. She applied for a grant that funded work in India. "I spent a year there questioning and learning how people rebuild their houses after a disaster. When I saw that they were not rebuilding them with safer layouts, that's when I decided to start my own organization to help these people build more earthquake-resistant homes."

After her trip to India, Elizabeth returned home and started applying for additional grants to help get her idea off the ground, eventually securing the seed money she needed to get her project going—and just in time. Soon afterward, the tsunami in Indonesia hit the coast, killing thousands of people and displacing whole communities.

Elizabeth and her team set up shop for the first time, making lots of mistakes, miscalculating the magnitude of her job, but learning valuable lessons about what worked best and what didn't work at all. They ended up building 33 houses by hiring local builders, and then partnered with other organizations to help build more than 4,000 earthquake-resistant buildings.

Flush from her success, Elizabeth next started a program in Sumatra to help rebuild after severe earthquakes had devastated the country. People were receiving some government assistance to rebuild their homes, so Elizabeth began advising them about how to build earthquake-resistant structures. "We were sharing basic knowledge, like when you wet a brick before you build a wall, it makes [the wall] much stronger."

Once she developed her model, Elizabeth moved to Peru to start the same sort of program, teaching local people how to prevent future disasters by building structures that are sturdier. She now has plans to keep her project going all over the globe.

Looking back on the last few years since she got out of school, Elizabeth is amazed at what she's been able to accomplish. She had always envisioned that it was the social work or disaster relief or health professions that were involved in promoting social justice issues. She never dreamed that as an engineer, she, too, could become involved helping people in so many neglected regions of the world. It is a lesson that applies to all of us—no matter what your field of interest or specialty, there is *always* something that you can do to be of service to those who need us the most.

For Elizabeth, it all began with taking risks, trying some things that she wasn't sure would work. "You have to be willing to take the next step. Get out into whatever field you're interested in and see what it's like. And move around. Especially in your 20s, you have so much time to experiment. Part of the process is trying something that fails, because then you can just go on to the next thing. Trying something that does not work also means going on to something that may work. Everything I've done has changed my path, but its brought me closer and closer to the perfect place to be, which is where I am right now."

ACCEPT UNCERTAINTY: ZANA BRISKI, KIDS WITH CAMERAS

This is another story of someone with a particular talent and interest who figured out a way to use her skills to help the most needy children in the world. Like the others we are profiling, Zana's organization was hardly planned strategically, but rather sprang from experiences she fell into.

Growing up, Zana always had a passion for photography. Ever since she was a child, she spent time developing photos in her cousin's basement darkroom, which sparked a lifelong passion for capturing images of people. It was this same interest that sparked another strong interest in the plight of women around the world. After she learned about the ways that girls were marginalized in India, to the point of female infants being murdered, she decided to go there to see for herself what she might do. She wanted to use her skills as a photographer to increase awareness of the problems there. Without any contacts or knowing anyone at all, Zana just showed up in Calcutta, where she spent several months visiting clinics, hospitals, and charities that were trying to address the ways that women and girls were being neglected and abused.

Once her own financial resources were depleted, Zana returned home to fund another trip to India, this time learning about the "red light" district in Calcutta where all the brothels were located. "I had a deep gut reaction to the red light district, so I spent the next couple of years trying to gain access to it, spending six months out of each year in India. I never had any funding for this; most of it I just put on credit cards."

Zana was not just interested in taking photographs of the street people to further her own career; she was determined to do something to help them. Photographers and journalists are taught at every stage of their training not to get involved with their subjects, to remain objective and detached; it isn't their job to save people, but rather to record their experiences and let others lend a hand. But with everything she had seen, Zana could no longer remain a bystander. She had to do something.

With no experience or funding, Zana's first attempt to start an organization in Calcutta failed miserably, in large part because she was trying to provide small loans to people but didn't really understand the system. She was heartbroken but not discouraged. She would try again, and this time she would launch a project more directly related to her own area of expertise—photography.

"I started to notice that all of the children were always grabbing at my camera. They loved taking pictures with it, and that's when I really wanted to see the world through their eyes and empower them to take their own pictures of the world around them."

Zana also felt the children's pictures could be used to help drive awareness of their poverty. "Right from the start, I wanted to make a book from their work, to sell it, have the proceeds help the kids, and eventually get them out of the brothels where their mothers worked as prostitutes."

Zana's plan was incredibly simple—and inspired. She went home and bought a suitcase of point-and-shoot cameras, then returned to Calcutta to teach the children who lived in brothels to use them. From the very first lessons, she realized that something amazing was happening. The kids loved to run around taking pictures, recording what they saw, then meeting with Zana afterwards to review their work. They felt important and valued.

If this wasn't a crazy enough idea, then the next stage was even more audacious. Zana's boyfriend at the time was a documentary filmmaker, so she invited him to join her on the next trip to India. Maybe this could bring even more awareness to the plight of the children and their mothers.

The footage of Zana teaching the kids how to take pictures and trying to get them out of the brothels was eventually turned into a documentary that was soon to become an international phenomenon. "Right from the first screening at Sundance [Film Festival], we knew we were onto something very special. People were crying and it became clear that this film could be a tremendous tool for change."

The film *Born into Brothels* eventually went on to win Documentary of the Year at the 2004 Academy Awards, launching Zana and her efforts on a massive, international scale, eventually consuming her life. To help take advantage of all this publicity, Zana started a foundation to help raise money for the kids, even though she had no prior experience in this area. "I went out and bought the book *Nonprofit for Dummies*, found a lawyer who would do pro bono work, and got the organization up and running. The idea was to take the model that I used in Calcutta and inspire this work to happen all over the world."

With her success in India, Zana decided to expand her helping efforts to Africa, addressing issues of climate change, which has always interested her. People often ask why she has moved on from something that has been so successful to start over again. "When I originally moved to Calcutta, people thought I was nuts. But then after the film it all made sense. It seems crazy to a lot of people, but I just continue to follow my intuition and don't listen to what other people say. Sometimes it's difficult, but I couldn't imagine another way to live."

Zana believes that the most important thing that anyone can do is to follow his or her own path rather than somebody else's, even if others disagree. "If I had listened to all the people around me, or needed to know exactly what was going to happen, I would have never begun these projects. I had no idea what I was doing my whole time in India, but I showed up, gave myself to the experience and put one foot in front of the other. Sometimes you just have to jump in, look for signs, and accept that you won't know everything that will happen."

STAY OPEN: SAM GOLDMAN, D.LIGHT

Sam Goldman could be a described as a true citizen of the world. His parents worked for an American relief agency so Sam grew up on several continents. He spent his elementary school years living in Pakistan until the Gulf War began and they had to flee for their lives. His family next moved to Peru, where he learned how much people of his own country were despised by local people. "They hated Americans there. We had to live with a wire fence around our house, and sometimes I would be playing video games with my friends and I could hear a bomb that went off when the terrorists bombed the Pizza Hut or something like that."

Sam went to high school in India before beginning college in Canada. "That was the first time I started trekking and really getting to know environmental issues. I was into all the outdoor clubs and really trying to find a way to protect the outdoor space and biodiversity. I was a vegan, turning off our lights every three seconds, and very conscious of environmental issues. And during my summer breaks I would go visit my parents, who were living in Rwanda as directors of the aid effort there during the genocide that was happening."

Sam Goldman is the founder of d.light, a company devoted to bringing environmental sustainable energy to developing countries.

Upon finishing college, Sam wasn't quite sure what he wanted to do. After growing up with parents who were traveling the world to help the most unfortunate people, he just couldn't imagine himself working a regular job. But neither did he have much interest in following in the exact footsteps of his parents. He needed to find his own path that reflected his interests and goals.

Just about the time that Sam was going to join the Peace Corps, he met some friends from college who were planning a bike trip across Canada to raise awareness about global warming. Sam and 30 others biked across the continent, stopping at community centers and mayors' offices along the way to educate people and politicians about what they could do to conserve energy and reduce their consumption.

During the bike trip, Sam received repeated calls from the Peace Corps, saying that they were prepared to send him to a small African country he had never heard of, Bennin, that was located somewhere near Nigeria. Although it was a small nation, he learned that there were 70 different languages spoken there.

Sam found himself living in a traditional village with no running water or electricity. "Then I realized that the Peace Corps is not as much of a developmental agency as it is a cross-cultural exchange, and that developmental work was what I really wanted to do. During my stay there I got really into building things. I would try to make better latrines for the people in the village, and specially shaped jars that would help women with their drinking water. During that whole process I learned that I just loved masonry, designing products, and building."

Even though he was working outside of his assigned mandate and jobs, Sam helped the local people start an orphanage and then tried to begin sustainable farming and commercial enterprises so the people could improve their economic conditions. During these attempts, he realized that was completely out of his league, with no idea what he was doing. He might like to build things, but he had no training in commerce or business. The obvious next step was to apply to business school.

"People say how hard the Stanford University application process is, but at least most people have electricity when they are doing it. They wanted me to take the GMAT [business admission test], but I wrote them a letter saying that the closest place to take the GMAT was 800 miles away, much of it by foot! They still said that I had to take the test, so my girlfriend and I went on a month-long motorcycle trip to get to the testing center. I studied on the way out there but when we arrived, it wasn't even operating. Fortunately, they set it up for us the next day."

Graduate school opened a whole new world for Sam, teaching him about global issues and how to think on a much bigger scale. "It totally changed the way I looked at life. But coming in there, I didn't know squat about squat. There were all these insanely intelligent people and I was just coming off of living in a very nonacademic village environment."

Product design courses attracted Sam the most, especially those that were focused on developing countries. As part of the class, Sam was paired with a team of students to actually create a product that could add value to the developing world. Sam had some inside advantage here, having grown up in those environments for much of his life.

"During my four years in the Peace Corps, I went to Macedonia twice to visit my parents. It was there that I first discovered LED [light emitting diode] lamps. They were amazing, because they only cost a dollar, but they were way better than using a kerosene lamp, which was what most people did. When I went back to my village, I would always have a little one in my house, and it would kick the crap out of the kerosene. At that time, I realized this could be a really big deal for the developing world. But I didn't really know what to do about it."

That discovery was the perfect idea for his class's project. "I knew it could work because I had lived it. So we got our team together and made a really jinky prototype over the course of the semester and tested it in southeast Asia. We got good feedback, and finally presented the product at the end of the class."

When the class ended, different members of that team went off to work at various summer jobs—one at Google, another at Apple. Sam went to work for Wal-Mart. "A friend of mine worked for an environmental consulting group that was helping Wal-Mart adapt environmentally sustainable practices. So she put me in touch with the head of environmental sustainability at Wal-Mart, and I was really impressed."

Sam's friends thought that he had totally sold out going to work for the biggest of big, impersonal corporations. "Even I hated Wal-Mart. All that energy I put into hating Wal-Mart, if I had just gone and talked to five employees, I could have made a much more educated assessment of the company. That's what I got to do from the inside. So I ended up being in this company that I thought I was going to hate, and it ended up being more progressive than anything I had ever seen. And they were impacting the world on a huge level, because they were becoming committed to recycling and other issues on a scale that only they could reach. They were bringing in Al Gore and other environmental leaders to consult. It was exciting to affect that kind of change on a massive scale."

Rather than continuing with corporate America after graduation, Sam reassembled his team to see if they could get the lamp idea off the ground. They recruited engineers to help with product design. They applied for grants to raise seed money. They even found a venture capital firm that agreed to sponsor them, bringing in other investors.

"The thing that I learned in design school is to prototype everything. Find a way to rapidly prototype whatever it is you want to do and refine what it is you're aiming at. For example, if I wanted to design a telephone, I wouldn't try to define what the end product looks like. I would go out and talk to 15 people and ask them what communications and telephones mean to them. Then I would just go watch people communicate with each other. Then I would do a mock up of a telephone and interact with people with that. Rather than just trying to design the perfect phone, break it down into smaller steps."

That has been Sam's motto throughout life—trying to make products better and more adaptable so they can be used within environments that have few resources. Sam credits his schooling around the world, which taught him to remain open to new and different possibilities, to live with inherent contradictions.

Half the world has no access to electricity, so Sam is determined to find a way to literally provide light in their lives. His goal is no less than to replace every kerosene lamp in the world, replacing them with affordable, safer, sustainable alternatives.

What made it possible for Sam, or anyone else, to implement such a grand scheme? For one thing, it was recognizing that his good intentions and motivation were not nearly enough. He also needed knowledge, skills, and networks that he didn't have to make his vision become a reality.

THE WORLD IS YOUR OYSTER: JESSICA MAYBERRY, VIDEO VOLUNTEERS

Many of the people we have profiled so far were exposed to global issues from an early age, living abroad with parents who became models for promoting social justice. But if someone had told Jessica Mayberry while she was growing up that someday she'd be living in India running her own nonprofit group, she would have never believed it.

Jessica wanted to work in the media after graduation, so she moved to New York to work for the major television networks. "I quickly found out that mainstream TV was not very interesting, it was all reality stuff. It also had a major lack of international perspective, and I found this very inward looking."

While she quickly became disillusioned with the industry, Jessica began to see the potential that new technologies were bringing, providing more power for the independent filmmaker. "I began to notice that any young person could just grab a camera and do video journalism. So I took a weekend course in making films and just fell in love with it."

While Jessica began to nurture her interest in film, she also wanted to do something relevant overseas. "I started contacting different non-governmental organizations (NGOs) in India, saying 'I know how to make films,' which I totally didn't know how to do yet. But I realized that they really needed volunteers to help them make films about the social issues they were trying to address."

Jessica was accepted to work at a foundation in India and ended up moving to Ahmadabad, the country's unofficial capitol for NGOs. "One of my first journal entries said, 'What if I was here for the rest of my life?' And I'm still here today!"

Jessica ended up spending nine months at one of the biggest NGOs in India, which had a unit that focused on making films about different issues. "By the time I left them, I had an inkling of an idea, which ended up becoming Video Volunteers. I realized that lots of NGOs wanted to create films about their issues, but they couldn't afford to make them. So I knew that if I could bring over filmmaker volunteers to help these NGOs, it would be very well received."

Jessica went back to America with her inkling of an idea and met a woman by the name of Kathy Eldon. Kathy was the mother of Dan Eldon, a 22-year old lawyer/photojournalist who had been killed in Somalia. Kathy published her son's journal; the book was featured on *Oprah* and was a huge inspiration to millions of people.

Kathy ended up becoming Jessica's fiscal sponsor, helping raise enough money to get Jessica's project off the ground. "For the first couple of years, we sent about 20 filmmakers to different organizations to make films to support their efforts. But people would only stay for two months and then go back to their own jobs. We then asked ourselves, 'How do we make this more permanent?' That's when we started to train members of the local Indian community to become filmmakers and tell their own stories."

That evolution of Jessica's original idea has now resulted in the empowerment of 80 local video makers spread out all across India, each one producing their own video news magazines that they show in their local villages. More than just providing authentic content for the community, Video Volunteers is also a massive source of empowerment for the people who are trained to become filmmakers. "What happens if these people are given the same kind of skills that filmmakers from the BBC or NYU Film School receive? When you give these people this opportunity, and put them through 18 months of intensive film training, they end up producing the most powerful work we have seen."

Jessica is amazed by the progress. The original batch of filmmakers, who have only been working for two years, are already producing documentaries about poverty, water, and all the other issues that impact them the most. "It's hard, but it's very rewarding. Two years ago we would have never imagined we would have gotten to where we are now; last month we managed to raise over a million dollars, and when we started out I didn't even know how I was going to cover my travel expenses.

"This all seems so far away from where I grew up and how I lived. It's such a privilege that I can be a part of these people's lives in this intense way. I think I came over here wanting to understand why the world is like it is. Why we in America have so much, while people in the rest of the world have so little. I don't have an answer to that question yet, but I feel like I'm being a part of these people's lives and helping to make change."

FINDING YOUR OWN PATH

In this first set of stories, which focus on global issues addressed by those working abroad, we are particularly impressed with the range of interests and fields that are represented. Regardless of your own field of interest—in the sciences, social sciences, humanities, arts, health, education, engineering, or business—there is room for anyone to use their skills and talents to assist those who are most in need.

Although one of the people whose stories we presented had training in public health, the others we profiled were a photographer, filmmaker, business entrepreneur, and engineer. Several of them were exposed to a "jet-setting" lifestyle early in life because their families lived and worked abroad, but others in this chapter and the following chapters lived rather sheltered lives and were only exposed to the needs of the developing world after reaching college.

We move next to individuals who have chosen to work within their local communities to make a difference. Indeed, it isn't necessary to travel more than a few miles from your home to find people who have been neglected, marginalized, or abused.

CHAPTER 13

Local Community Activists

Do you have to be an international jet setter to change the world? If that's a path that piques your interest, then go for it. But for many others, starting locally in your own community is the best place to begin. It is likely that your college has established programs with community agencies, service learning or internship opportunities, even independent studies that you can arrange through supervision of a favored instructor.

You don't need to look far to find people in need and lives that could be changed for the better. Even in the wealthiest nations on Earth, poverty plagues a large number of people, and disparity between classes is a serious issue.

In this chapter, we profile several individuals who have worked to make a difference in their communities, starting out small and modest and growing their projects into larger enterprises. Lest you think that you have to be older and experienced to make something like this happen, our youngest subject was only 13 years old!

These are the stories of people who have a passion for social justice and put that passion to work in their local communities. They were courageous and bold, and their impact is long lasting. They didn't have to go across the globe to begin their work; instead they started with what was directly in front of them and went from there.

LEARN TO LISTEN: AARON BARTLEY, PUSH BUFFALO

How did a kid from Buffalo become one of the most effective labor movement organizers of his generation? For Aaron Bartley, it's been about being attentive and humble enough to listen to the people around him talk about what bothers them most. "There's always this tension in activism between humility and a sort of stubbornness," Aaron explains, "but you have to find a way to represent both of those things. If you don't find that side of humility, you're not going to be sincere in your work."

Unlike the people in the previous chapter who grew up with models of what they wanted to be, Aaron's ambition to become a community activist and labor organizer didn't arise until after he left school. "I had an internship right after college working through the labor union that threw me right into one of the most exciting labor movements in quite a while, called 'Justice for Janitors' in Denver. We worked to organize janitors and help them get better wages. It was there that I saw how activism could be more than just a symbolic gesture. I was brainwashed in school to think that activists were marginal players and not part of the real game. So that was very important for me to see that organizing and activism could be very structured and could lead to measurable, concrete change."

During that labor campaign, Aaron was introduced to some leaders in the field, one a tactical genius who was a master at applying pressure through appropriate, measured, yet powerful forms of civil disobedience, marches, strikes, whatever it took to get the job done and bring people's attention to the plight of workers. A second mentor had skills recruiting and working with "power players," those who were in the best positions to make decisions and affect outcomes.

Aaron went on to work for a few other local activist networks, refining his organizational skills and learning how to motivate people to get involved in a common cause. Hungry for more knowledge about the legal system and how it could be used to promote greater social justice among the poor, Aaron went to law school at the most elite institution in the country. Until this time, he'd been spending time with the working poor, so he was appalled at the injustices he saw right on campus at Harvard, in which custodial workers and other service personnel felt marginalized. "I heard again and again about many Haitian and other immigrants who had to live an hour away from the university, working two jobs, 90 hours a week, just to survive. It was evident that something needed to be done."

Aaron used his organizing skills to start a labor movement at Harvard. "Every month we would take some sort of action. One time, on admissions day for new freshman, we took over the Admissions Department hallway in a pretty militant, but nonviolent, way and told the stories of workers who cleaned that hallway. Sometimes the workers who cleaned those hallways would come out and tell their stories directly."

"We got to the point where we had more than 200 people showing up at these monthly events pretty regularly. We had Cornell West coming out. Once Matt Damon and Ben Affleck came out, and Ben told the story of his own father, who was also a janitor. We did this for about two years, holding 25 rallies, but still the administration was not willing to discuss these issues with us. We were fighting to create a commission that would draft a report highlighting the labor situation at Harvard."

After two years of hard work, Aaron and his supporters occupied the President's office for 21 straight days in a sit-in. "When we took that action, we were pretty uncertain as to how it would turn out. We didn't know if we would be alienating and pushing away the 80% of the student body who was not engaged in our effort and whose support we needed. But it basically went the other way. The sit-in brought huge crowds of support from students, faculty members, and workers who came out every day. It became a sort of festival with a rally happening in Harvard Yard each morning and a vigil scheduled each evening. People brought tents into Harvard Yard and were just camping out. It turned into this huge chaotic thing, and the media covered everything. All of that pressure caused the administration to finally negotiate with our group."

Aaron's efforts eventually paid off, and the administration agreed to provide better compensation and working conditions for the employees. It wasn't like they didn't have the money, with their billions of dollars in endowments, but someone just needed to get their attention that this was a cause worth supporting.

After Harvard, Aaron stayed and worked in Boston for three years doing much the same kind of work on other local campuses like Boston College, Boston University, and Northeastern University. He made some headway in these efforts, but he felt that his hometown of Buffalo was calling to him for help. Buffalo is an industrial city in upstate New York that has been plagued by factory closings, rampant unemployment, and serious poverty issues. Three quarters of all the factory jobs disappeared within a few years, the result of outsourcing jobs abroad.

Aaron moved back to Buffalo "without much of a plan," and started PUSH (People United for Sustainable Housing) Buffalo to help develop local projects in communities that have been virtually ignored. "We take abandoned properties and renovate them to higher standards. Every worker comes out of that neighborhood." At the time of this interview, they'd completed six units. They plan to complete another 20 in the next 18 months.

When it comes to offering advice for how others can find their way, Aaron has some reassuring words. "I would say just take a deep breath. Remember that you are your own person. Every one of your friends might be interviewing for Goldman Sachs or some other big firm, but if you don't know what you want to do, I really respect people who do their own thing and work as a substitute teacher for a year or in a restaurant. And while you're doing that, meet like-minded people in your community and try to understand the activism that's happening."

Aaron acknowledges that there is tremendous family and social pressure to get a job that fits certain expectations. You are supposed to go after the highest possible salary and search for a job that gives you the best chance to rise up the promotional ladder. But often, people who have followed that path don't necessarily find their work fulfilling and meaningful.

DON'T BE AFRAID TO CHANGE: FARAJII MUHAMMAD, NEW LIGHT LEADERSHIP COALITION

Farajii grew up in a middle class area of Baltimore and had ambitions to someday become an actor. To help him achieve this goal, he applied to the prestigious Baltimore School for the Arts, and was accepted. "That school really opened up my eyes to a lot of things. It's where I started to evolve into a person."

The campus was located in downtown Baltimore, so Farajii had to take a 45-minute bus ride every day to get to school. The bus went through some parts of town where "young people didn't have the chance to take advantage of the same opportunities that I was having in college. So on those bus rides I started to ask myself. 'How important is it for me to just go off to Hollywood but not help other people along the way?'"

This was a moment of awakening for Farajii, in that he made a decision to put his acting career on hold and take a different path toward serving humankind in a more direct way. He wasn't sure where this would lead him, but he was willing to trust his intuition that this would be his path in life. "I knew that something had to be done, I just didn't know how to do it."

Around that time, Farajii met his future wife, Tamara. He was 19 and she was 17. Part of their attraction was shared interests in what they could do in their community, where young people didn't have a strong voice.

Tamara and Farajii realized that there was no youth-focused organization in Baltimore that was actually led by young people. They wondered how these so-called youth organizations could really help the next generation if young people were not actually involved in decision making.

To get their organization off the ground, Farajii and Tamara had to leverage each other's strengths and learn how to divide up the roles for their effort. "Our skills blended really well together. When you start an organization with someone else, you want to find someone who can complement your skill sets, and you need to establish roles early on so there is an understanding that you play in different areas, but that you're still on the same page. This process has been reflected in the growth of our organization."

Tamara was the business mind behind their effort, having some experience in that domain, while Farajii used his acting skills to become the public face of the organization. One of the first things they did was to create a national leadership summit to attract young people to their movement. They ended up recruiting more than 100 high school students to sign up. "I'll never forget leaving the conference that night and having an overwhelming sense of accomplishment, because we did something that we had set out to do."

After that first organizational meeting, the real work started to happen. "After the event, I was excited, but I was also nervous, because we knew we had to do something more, but there was no one showing us where to go. We had to walk by faith and not by sight."

They decided to expand the organization into training, so that they could have a more permanent institution in the community. This involved developing a curriculum that prepared young people for leadership positions, not only in Baltimore but throughout the Atlantic coast.

The rewards for Farajii have been much deeper than he ever imagined. "You can't put a monetary value on what it's like to do this work—it's a priceless feeling. The other day, Tamara and I were at this function, and one of the parents came up to us and said that her daughter had gone through our program. She told us how thankful she was that her daughter was a part of our effort and that now she is talking about going to college and has a new outlook on life. When I heard that, and saw the joy coming out of her eyes, it just blew me away."

As excited as he feels, Farajii is also humbled by the work and its value in people's lives. The process can be tedious and tiresome, but you know that when you are touching someone else's life you are changing the world. And that's a beautiful thing."

OVERCOME YOUR FEARS: KYRA BOBINET, VISION YOUTHZ

When Kyra Bobinet was growing up, she was involved in a number of volunteer projects, including raising money for the Special Olympics, volunteering with autistic youth, and working with pregnant teenage girls. She had a passion for community service, but as she grew older her focus changed to science. She eventually went on to study at one of the nation's top medical schools, but she began to question what her purpose might be in life. "It was nagging at me that I was just on autopilot, studying medicine."

Many decisions we make in life are incremental, made gradually over a long period of time without our conscious awareness; others are sudden, dramatic, and hit us when we are least expecting it. On Martin Luther King Day, Kyra had an experience that inspired her to refocus her path. "I had just come home from a ski trip and began to feel a drumming message coming out of me, one that inspired me to write out this whole new path for my life. It involved letting go of my own plans for medicine and starting to advocate on behalf of disenfranchised people."

This realization was not exactly easy to put into action, because it meant completely changing her life plan, not to mention disappointing people who had certain expectations for her, which she was now cancelling. At this time, she was president of her class and achieving at the highest level in one of the most competitive arenas. "So here I am, 24 years old, and on one hand I'm really excited to lead this new path, but on the other hand, I'm thinking 'Great, this sucks.'"

Kyra Bobinet left an extremely lucrative career in medicine to follow her passion and start an organization that helps youth leaving juvenile detention facilities to gain life skills for the real world.

During medical school, Kyra had volunteered at juvenile hall and was inspired by the young men she met there. "The guys were the draw. They were brilliant and inspiring. The experience made me determined to do something for them, and I began to realize that there was no support structure in place to help these kids assimilate back into the world once they were released. They weren't receiving any training in mainstream life skills, and as a result, a majority of those guys being released would return to juvenile hall."

When Kyra graduated from medical school, rather than applying for a lucrative medical residency, she applied for an Echoing Green Fellowship to help start Vision Youthz. This was an organization that began in her living room. "I had never started anything of that magnitude and complexity before. It felt like we were on a small-craft boat out on the open ocean swimming against all the forces."

In addition to the struggle of starting a grassroots organization, Kyra had to also face tension from her family. "It was a huge financial struggle. I had a family and my husband was very angry at me for not becoming a doctor. His take on it was that I was being selfish, but my take on it was that I was transcending selfishness."

The experience of building Vision Youthz produced both incredible joy, as well as pain. "We would lose a young man about every year to murder, which is shocking in a small, tight-knit organization like ours. But then something great would happen: five of our guys would graduate from high school, or someone would go on to college. The point where I felt the most accomplished was when I stepped out of the Executive Director role after 11 years, and we had lowered recidivism (juvenile hall re-entry rates) from 80% to 25% in San Francisco County."

One thing that helped Kyra persist through all the trials associated with her work was meditation. "My singular advice to anyone is to have a meditation practice. It's not a spiritual thing, it's a cognitive skill, and it's a life raft for doing any kind of intense work. It causes you to know your thoughts, understand what is happening inside your head, and to observe those things mindfully."

So after 11 years of leading Vision Youthz, Kyra felt it was time to pass the reins to the very skilled staff who could continue the work. "I'm half Native American, and I take an annual solo 'vision quest,' where I live in nature by myself. I invite silence, and in that silence, the vision for what I am to do next comes to me." That is how she found her next path.

Today Kyra is attending graduate school, where she is studying public health. "It's a tool and a skill that will allow me to reincarnate in a larger way, moving as a broader trainer where I can spread concepts and practices that will help people who are serving others. It's the next development stage for me."

"My path has been about learning to follow my nose so that I can constantly be in that moment of flow. It's like surfing and suspending that moment where the wave finally catches you. And once you're fully engaged, you've found the sweet spot of your own existence."

You can certainly hear the courage in each of these stories. Aaron, Farajii, and Kyra each chose paths that went against what was expected of them. In these brief narratives, it seems as if they simply decided what they wanted to do—and then did it. But you can also sense the confusion and uncertainty they faced. Imagine the disapproval and scolding they must have heard from family and friends who wanted them to purse a different, more conventional and safe agenda. Consider the disappointment and despair they encountered when their initial efforts were rebuffed or outright rejected. Imagine the discomfort they had to put up with, surrendering many material comforts to promote their causes. And think about the frustration they experienced feeling so far in over their heads most of the time, working in areas they knew so little about. This is all part of the journey, facets that are further echoed in the stories that follow.

CHAPTER 14

Thinking Globally, Acting Locally

Rather than choosing between working locally or globally, in this new, progressive world, why not define your own path based on what you're most passionate about? Do you love basketball? Then start a "Shoot-a-Thon" to raise money for children orphaned by AIDS in Zimbabwe. Want to help bring a source of modest funding to budding entrepreneurs in the developing world? Start your own web site and connect would-be lenders with those in desperate need of resources to get their dream off the ground. In this chapter, you'll read about the innovative ideas from people who simply defined something they were passionate about and then leveraged advances in technology and popular culture to bring their visions to life.

REBOUND: AUSTIN GUTWEIN, HOOPS OF HOPE

When life doesn't go your way, sometimes it's hard to bounce back. But if a nine-year old kid can do it, maybe anyone else can too. When Austin Gutwein didn't make his school basketball team, he didn't just stop there. He knew there was something more he could do with his passion, something that could end up having a far greater impact on the world. He started an organization called Hoops of Hope, whose mission can be summarized by the opening statement on its web site:

> This is Chris.
> He is 3 years old.
> Last year he lost his parents to AIDS.

If you could save a child from becoming an orphan,
By doing something as simple as shooting free throws,
Would you?

Hoops of Hope is now the biggest basketball shoot-a-thon in the country. It operates like a walk-a-thon or jog-a-thon, but is focused on Austin's passion for basketball. Over the last four years, Hoops of Hope has raised $325,000 to build a school and medical clinic and to help sponsor many children who have lost their families to AIDS.

If Austin had given up on his passion after not making the school basketball team, hundreds of kids wouldn't be getting an education, many people in

Austin Gutwein, age 13, turned his love of basketball into a whole organization to raise hundreds of thousands of dollars to support orphans in Africa.

Zimbabwe would not have access to health care, and Austin would not have become the inspirational 13-year-old he is today.

When you think of people who are significantly impacting the lives of children in third-world countries, you often don't imagine that that person is also a kid. Austin Gutwein debunks that notion pretty quickly and believes that children really can change the world and make it better. Repeating a theme you've heard previously from our adult stories, Austin said, "As kids we shouldn't wait until we're adults to make a difference. You just need to find something you're passionate about and not get nervous about what other people might think."

At age nine, Austin and his family sponsored a child in Africa through the World Vision program. As part of the package, World Vision sent them an informational video about one of Africa's most alarming crises: children who were being orphaned at an alarming rate because their parents were dying of AIDS. "I remember we received this video in the mail, and honestly, that changed me forever. I'm different because of it now. It showed this kid named Maggie who had to end up living with her great-grandma because her parents died of AIDS. Night after night for a few months I just kept thinking what my life would be like without my parents. How could kids go through that?' Then I started asking my dad if there was something I could do to help these kids."

Dan Gutwein, Austin's father, hooked him up with a representative from World Vision to talk things through, and Austin remembers the advice that the guy gave him. "He encouraged me to use what I love to make a difference. At that point I loved basketball, so I thought maybe I could do something with that to help these kids."

Then 10 years old, Austin decided to do a type of jog-a-thon, but instead of running laps around a track, he would shoot free throws. Later that year, he ended up shooting 2,057 free throws, which resulted in raising more than $3,000 to sponsor some children in Africa. "When I told my parents I wanted to do it again the next year, they were kind of surprised because they thought it was a one-time event. But then the next year we had over 1,000 kids come out, each of whom ended up shooting 1,000 free throws."

Those 100,000 free throws ended up netting over $35,000 for World Vision, who would use the funds to help children affected by AIDS. But Austin still knew that he could do more. "The next year, I told my dad that I wanted to do something more tangible, something that I could really see and feel. So we asked World Vision if there was another project we could do. They said that they were trying to raise money to build a school in Africa."

Now that Austin had his mission, he organized the third year of his event. This time he recruited 1,400 children to each shoot 1,000 free throws, raising over $100,000 for the school. Austin traveled all the way to Zimbabwe to visit the project that he helped create. "I don't know how to explain it—it's just so hard to describe. It wasn't as much rewarding as it was just amazing. To just know that these kids are going to be able to go to school for the first time and get an education. Just to see the smiles on their faces for something like building a school, I will never forget that."

As you can imagine, visiting Africa for the first time at 13 years old had a profound impact on Austin. "My most memorable experience was just hanging out with the kids. They are just like me, but they're living in poverty. To experience all of that was totally life changing." This only inspired him to work harder for his cause, this time recruiting more than 5,000 children to participate.

By this time, Hoops of Hope had grown into an international organization, with events happening in 85 locations and 5 countries around the world. The goal this year was to raise $150,000 to help build a medical lab in Zimbabwe. Austin explained, "The people who had AIDS in Zimbabwe couldn't get medical treatment. So we thought, rather than helping the kids who were left behind when their parents died of AIDS, let's try to prevent their parents from dying in the first place." More than $200,000 was raised, and the medical center is currently being constructed.

Austin has been receiving quite a bit of media attention lately. He was featured on MSNBC and CBS Sports, where Ashley Judd narrated his story. "All of the media stuff has not changed me at all. What's changed me is meeting those kids in Africa. It's amazing what kids can do when they're given the opportunity to make a difference."

GETTING VULNERABLE: MATTHEW AND JESSICA FLANNERY, KIVA

If you know you want to make a difference in the world, and you believe you have the ability to create that change, how do you react in the face of those struggles once you encounter them? Jessica and Matthew Flannery,

Matthew and Jessica Flannery *originally started Kiva to provide small business loans, sometimes in increments of just $25, to entrepreneurs in the developing world. Since then, they've raised over $25,000,000 and have started a microlending movement.*

the founders of Kiva, believe you have to get vulnerable, and get as close as possible to the people you're trying to impact: "Peel away the boundaries between you and the people you want to work with," Jessica advocates. "If you do that peeling, you can build connections that change you and change the world. In the course of peeling away those boundaries, you become vulnerable. Don't fight it. Strive for vulnerability—beautiful things can happen out of it" (Katz, 2007).

The Flannerys see their organization, Kiva, as the solution to a marriage problem. It might sound a little strange to start an international social movement to address problems in their relationship, but that is exactly what happened.

"A few months before Matt and I got engaged, we were in a pre-engagement course at our church. Every week we would come together with a half-dozen other couples to talk about different life issues. One time it was career-day, so we came in and talked about our career vision and where we wanted to live."

That's when things got a little interesting. Matt confessed that his vision was to work for one of the technology start-ups in Silicon Valley that lead to zillions of dollars in stock options. It was Jessica's turn after that and she admitted that her plan was to work on microfinance and go live in Africa. "There was a deafening silence in the room," Jessica recalls with a laugh, "because everyone realized, including us, that we had a problem."

Matthew and Jessica went ahead with the wedding, figuring that somehow they'd find a compromise. Then, six months into their marriage, Jessica was offered her dream job: to go work in East Africa for an organization called Village Enterprise Fund that distributes hundred dollar microlending grants for new businesses in Kenya, Uganda, and Tanzania.

Meanwhile, Matt had followed his own dream and was working for a tech firm in Northern California, just like he planned. During his first trip to visit Jessica in Africa, he was hooked. Combining their talents, they started a web site called Kiva, which means "unity" in Swahili. They contacted everyone on their wedding list, raising about $3,000 to help fund a handful of small businesses back in Uganda.

The basic idea was to help entrepreneurs in the developing world, such as a baker in Kenya or a carpenter in Tajikistan, gain access to small loans that could help grow their businesses. Leveraging the power of the Internet, their web site allowed the average Westerner to go online, review profiles of these entrepreneurs, and then directly lend them the funds right from their credit card, mostly in increments of just $25.

The idea of microlending was first pioneered by Muhammad Yunus (who eventually won the Nobel Prize for his work), but it had yet to be connected to the Internet, where average people could also get involved rather than just big banks.

"Jessica and I knew every business person on the web site for the first month," Matt said, "because they were all from the village in Uganda where she worked. We really just viewed it as a hobby at this stage. To everyone externally, we told them that we worked during the day at very serious jobs, and then just did this on the side."

One night, Matt and Jessica went out for dinner to eat Chinese food, and she threw a challenge on the table: "When are you going to quit your job and really do this with me? When are you going to take this seriously?"

Matt hesitated, chopsticks in midair, trying to figure out a way to stall. "I'll quit my job when Kiva hits a million dollars in loans."

"Uh huh," Jessica responded immediately, "but if you don't quit your job, how are you going to raise the million dollars?"

That got Matt's attention big time, so much so that the next week, when their work was featured on a well-known blog, he felt it was time to make his move and leave the safety of his secure and lucrative job for the great unknown.

On the day that Kiva was featured on the blog, more than 1,000,000 users flooded their site. "When I showed up to work that day," Matt remembered, "I had almost 1,000 e-mails in my inbox. That really changed my thinking. I thought, this wasn't just something that Jessica and I cared about, it was something that a *lot* of people might be able to get involved with."

Throughout the next few years, Kiva expanded very rapidly. They focused their mission (connecting people through lending for the sake of alleviating poverty), and raised more than $25,000,000, which went to help 16,000 small businesses in over 36 countries around the world.

Their business model is quite innovative. The loans require no collateral and have zero interest. Each payment is made through their web site, which processes all transactions without any fees. The average lender usually funds three different entrepreneurs at $25 each. That may only get you a night on the town in America, but in the developing world it can launch an entire business.

Kiva's operational costs are covered by donations from the lenders, so the company does not have to take a commission from the loans facilitated on the site. Throughout the course of the loan (usually 6 to 12 months) the lender receives e-mail journal updates from the sponsored entrepreneur. As the loans are repaid, the lenders eventually get all their money back.

The problem with the traditional child sponsorship model is how high the overhead is to manage that infrastructure. Because it leverages the power of the Internet, Kiva's infrastructure costs are extremely low, allowing about 90% of the funds to go directly to the entrepreneur.

What's most interesting of all is how this whole enterprise began as a very personal negotiation in their love relationship, how Matt and Jessica had to reconcile their different life values and ambitions in such a way that each would feel productive and useful. "Kiva married the high tech startup world with microfinance," Jessica summarized. "It was the perfect solution to Matt's and my relationship problem, and I can honestly say that it was born out of love" (Katz, 2007).

THINK VIRALLY: BLAKE MYCOSKIE, TOMS SHOES

After competing on CBS's *The Amazing Race* in 2002 (Blake and his sister Paige were four minutes away from winning the $1,000,000 prize), he vowed to return to his favorite countries he passed through all around the world. He was always literally running to the next place, competing with the clock, so he never had time to explore many of the countries he visited. He made a long list of the things he wanted to do: learn to sail in Brazil; play polo in Argentina; dive in Belize. There was nothing on his list about starting a new business.

Blake always had a strong desire to do something important for the world by using his passion for business. "When I was 19, I dropped out of college to start my own business, and a mentor gave me a piece of advice I will never forget: 'The more you give, the more you live.'"

While in Argentina learning to play polo, he noticed a number of people wearing the traditional Argentine shoes, the *alpargata*. Farmers had been wearing these lightweight, canvas slip-on shoes for more than one hundred years and they were becoming popular in mainstream Argentine culture as well. "I bought a few pairs and loved them. At the same time, I was struck by the terrible poverty in Argentina. Growing up in Texas, I had never seen anything like that. I met kids who would walk for miles just to fetch water or go to school. And many of the kids were actually turned away from school because they could not afford uniforms or shoes. They had cuts on their feet that would often go untreated and lead to serious medical problems—all because these kids didn't have any shoes!"

"I know it sounds cheesy, but I had an epiphany." Blake's vision was to start a company based on the principle of "one-to-one giving." For every pair of shoes he sold back in America, he would give another pair away to a third-world

Blake Mycoskie was a contestant on CBS's "The Amazing Race." When he returned to visit the countries he originally blitzed through during the show, he discovered a cause worth fighting for.

child in need. He started by bringing 200 shoes with him back to America. "My friends thought I was nuts. Here I was with all these shoes stuffed in my duffel bag, talking about a company that gives as much away as it sold. Looking back on it, it *was* pretty crazy, but excitement is contagious. I was so excited to tell people about the kids I met in Argentina that soon enough a few stores decided to give me a chance."

Blake went on to sell many more than 200 pairs of shoes. By 2006, he had sold more than 10,000 pairs, which resulted in a corresponding donation of

10,000 pairs of shoes to children back in Argentina. Later that year, the TOMS (Shoes for Tomorrow) team went on a shoe drop mission to South America to deliver all 10,000 pairs of shoes in person.

One team member recalls the powerful experience: "This little girl watched and eyed the bright pink pair of shoes I had in my hand. Her little black foot was sweaty from wearing an old holey pair of shoes, too small for her feet. I slipped the shoe on her foot, but it was tight. I could see she was surprised when I told her that I was going to get a pair that fit her. I reached in my bag and pulled out the next size up, which I slipped on her feet. They fit, and a big smile appeared on her beautiful face. I stood up handed her the old shoes and gave her a big hug. I held her and thought: The gift of TOMS to this child is an even greater gift to me."

Blake had no prior experience in fashion or the shoe industry, but "I always believed that if you are smart and willing to learn, you can accomplish anything. I started out by learning everything I could about fashion from my friends, and then just went from there."

The success of the shoe drop in Argentina led to more success back home. In 2007, musicians Isaac, Taylor, and Zac Hanson (of the band Hanson) partnered with TOMS after visiting Africa and seeing the effects of poverty. During their 2007 tour, the band walked with fans for one mile before each show, often barefoot, to raise awareness of this issue. Fans who participated were encouraged to buy TOMS shoes to support and help children in need of shoes. By November 2007, Hanson had done walks in 37 different cities, and TOMS were sold at every performance.

Then in October of 2007, the shoemaker with no prior fashion experience was awarded the "Peoples Design Award," presented by Smithsonian's Cooper-Hewitt during the annual National Design Awards Gala in New York City. Many national media publications caught wind of the growing enterprise, which drove awareness for the movement in all the major publications.

By the end of 2007, TOMS had sold enough shoes to prepare for its next shoe drop, this time in Africa, where they would give away 50,000 pairs of shoes. "We crisscrossed South Africa, going from Johannesburg to Port Elizabeth to Durban, stopping in many villages and townships along the way. We met kids in orphanages, schools, community centers, and alongside the road. My favorite moments were the mini shoe drops, where we would see kids selling pineapples or trinkets on the side of the road. Everyone would pile out of the vans and pair a child with a new pair of shoes. When I saw the joy on the children's faces, I knew that this is what I'm going to do for the rest of my life."

Blake believes that no matter what your age is, or your stage in life, everyone will eventually find their own calling—if they pay attention to what's going on around them and within them. "Originally, when I first dropped out of college, my philosophy was to be an entrepreneur and make a lot of money. Today, I don't want to be remembered for what I did, but what I gave away."

A student working in a remote village, providing support to children who would otherwise not remain in school.

FINDING YOUR OWN PASSION

We have presented more than a dozen examples, representing diverse ages, professions, contexts, geographic locations, and missions, all illustrating the different ways that people have tried to address social justice and human rights issues. If there are common themes that stand out in all these stories, it is that these people were all leading relatively ordinary lives, going about their businesses trying to get an education or find a suitable career. They were all restless and unsatisfied with following a traditional path, and so all took calculated risks to pursue a particular passion that gave their lives greater meaning and purpose.

We also hope you find it encouraging that none of these folks had any particular training or preparation (unlike you) to launch their projects. Most of them were rather naive and unaware of what would be involved or even how they would proceed. You may have noticed a parallel to our own stories as well, in that each of us stumbled and blundered into our callings, starting with very small steps that eventually grew into something much greater than we ever imagined. That is a theme we'd like to explore further in the next chapter: how you can do some of your best work in any domain by "going small" until you grow into something else that may very well capture your passion. "If you are excited enough about something," Blake Mycoskie summarized best, "you will learn everything you need to know along the way."

While we thoroughly endorse the value of enthusiasm and passion, there is also no substitute for experience and knowledge, the kind you get not only from the classroom but also, just as importantly, from working in the field. We hope we have inspired you to do something, somewhere, somehow, to make a difference, to use your talent and energy to help promote human rights and social justice for all people.

CHAPTER 15

Going Small

"Never doubt that a small group of thoughtful, committed citizens can change the world. Indeed, it's the only thing that ever has."

—Margaret Mead

This classic quote is perhaps even more relevant today than it was during her lifetime in the 20th century. Revolutions in technology, politics, and popular culture have democratized how the world operates in many ways. They have put more power in the hands of everyday people, giving them the tools to truly make a difference in the world. Any citizen of the world, armed with a mere keyboard, can launch messages into cyberspace that can have a huge impact on political or social movements.

You might presume from the title of this chapter that we think that going big—having grand schemes—is ill-advised. Not at all! Many large organizations are making a profound difference in the world through their efforts (think CARE, UNICEF, United Way, AID, Peace Corps). The large scale in which these groups can act brings massive assistance to people in need all across the globe.

Going small can also elicit powerful effects, especially when many people are collectively, passionately engaged in efforts for which they care deeply. All of those niches, often neglected or ignored by larger efforts, can be strung together to create an entirely new level of impact.

Today, the landscape for people who want to make a difference in the world has changed dramatically. New opportunities exist that weren't there for generations before us, empowering almost anyone to address issues that concern them in their neighborhoods, in their communities, or on the world stage. And these new developments are not just reserved for the major global players. For example, when my friends and I (Mike) started Roadtrip Nation after college, none of us had experience in filmmaking or starting grassroots organizations. I was a biology major with little experience in anything outside of a laboratory. I never thought I would end up filming a documentary that would result in an annual PBS series. In fact, if we had tried to do what we did even 10 years earlier, you could argue that it would have never gotten off the ground.

So it all begins with making that first, small effort, and noting the effects. If you like the outcome (and how it feels), do a little more of it; if you don't like what happened, then try something else.

ADVANCES IN TECHNOLOGY

People have been taking road trips for generations. But what was different about our first trip was that various technologies were just starting to emerge that would make it much easier to actually share what we were encountering on a very clear and visceral level. About the same time we hit the road, Sony came out with their new high quality digital camera, which was almost affordable if a bunch of young guys distributed the cost on all their credit cards. Little did we know that the footage we captured on the road using that camera (which we fondly named "Alberto") was actually television-quality images. Before that, any kind of video camera that was used for television was well beyond the budget of anyone other than a professional.

When we returned from our road trip and wanted to share our experiences, Apple had released their new film editing software, which made putting together our own documentary much easier than ever before—even amateurs like us could do it by reading a few books.

When more and more people began to learn about our road trip experiences, we needed something to showcase these lessons on a broader level. The Internet was the perfect tool for that, so we recruited some of our techie friends to help build our first web site. The web site and early documentary

I Just Don't Know How to Start

I've thought about starting my own non-profit to help the homeless in my local community, but I have no idea how to begin. Growing up, I had an uncle who was homeless, and he had a hard time figuring out where different shelters were to stay at on different nights. He would go from one shelter to the next, but when many of them were full, he would spend the entire night just searching for a place to sleep. If he would have just had a way of knowing which ones were full for the night, and which ones were open, he would have actually had a place to sleep many of those nights. It gets freezing here in the winter and knowing that he was out there on the streets really freaked me out. I've thought about starting a web site that could connect all the different shelters so they could better communicate with one another about their occupancy. That way all of the wandering homeless people would not have to be sitting in freezing lines just to see if they could have a bed for the night. I know the idea would work, but I just have no idea where to start. I have a few friends who have designed web sites. They've offered to help build the first site but I'm still trying to figure out how to put all the pieces together. I know I'll figure it out eventually but right now it's just taking a bit of time.

helped to build credibility, which led to some media coverage and our first book, increasing awareness of our project and its goals

Blake Mykoskie, the founder of TOMS Shoes, mentioned that his grassroots effort would not have been possible without leveraging new advances in technology. When he launched his first shoe drop to give shoes to thousands of children in Argentina, he posted videos from this experience on YouTube, which ended up receiving over 120,000 views! A similar thing happened with respect to our project in Nepal, in that Jeffrey learned to design the web site himself, with just a few hours of instruction, thereby making it possible for online readers to learn about what we were doing to help the neglected children and easily make contributions to support the work. Videos were also posted on YouTube to show potential donors the impact of their contributions.

Jessica and Matthew Flannery built upon Mohammad Yunus's concept of microfinance, which loans small amounts of capital to entrepreneurs in the developing world, by starting the Kiva web site, which allows anyone in the world (via any major credit card) to lend a baker in Tajikistan or a seamstress in Kenya the funds necessary to start their businesses and help themselves rise out of economic hardship.

As he leverages the Internet to help bring this vision to life, Matthew has an interesting vision for the future: "Our dream is that by 2017, there will be a fading distinction between what we call the third world and what we call the first world, between what we call the developing world and what we call the developed world. I already see this happening—there will be a leveling of the fields, and people will be able to interact as business partners. We will view people in Uganda as esteemed business partners, rather than people we need to take pity on."

CULTURAL ACCEPTANCE

As technology improves, and the playing field between the major experts and the everyday people with a dream is leveled, audiences have become accustomed to viewing experiences that are not as flashy, produced, or perfected.

I Have a Plan

Last summer I did a study abroad program in Romania and was stunned by how much child poverty there was on the streets. You always hear about the sketchy orphanages in Romania, but something I had not expected was to see how much worse it was for the kids on the streets. I tried to give them a few bucks here and there, even bought a few of them breakfast, but I just felt like there was something more that I could do. One idea I had was to go back there with a video camera and just record some of their stories. If people in the West had some idea of what these kids go through, they might be inspired to get involved, donate money, or just do something to help out. I've done some editing on my computer here and there, but this would be something on a whole new level, something more organized and with more purpose. I'm figuring out how to put this idea together now, finding the best camera to use and so on. And my plan is to save up enough to go back over there once I graduate next year, so I can make this documentary.

Even though it's hard to argue that reality television has helped American culture in any significant way, it has helped the mass public become comfortable with rougher content. PBS might not have aired our first *Roadtrip Nation* documentary even ten years earlier, because the viewing public were used to a very different quality of content: sitcoms with highly paid professional actors.

Zana Briski's effort benefited from the new reality television wave as well. Being a gifted photographer would not have been enough to promote her mission on behalf of children's and women's rights in India without new innovations to make cameras cheaper. When her grassroots documentary earned an Academy Award, widespread publicity made it possible for her cause to take off.

IT'S A SMALL WORLD

The world is indeed becoming more symbiotic, more interconnected, and less restricted by national borders. You read earlier about Sam Goldman, founder of d.light, who is leveraging these interconnections to bringing technology to underserved populations, including the 1.6 billion people who are currently living without electricity.

"I couldn't have created d.light even ten years ago," Sam admitted. "Everything about our business relies on the interconnected nature of the world. We currently have two people in California, one in Hong Kong, two in Shenzhen, China and one in New Delhi, India, all working together."

Sam and his international team hold their meetings via Skype, conduct board meetings via videoconference, and are constantly transferring designs and data across multiple time zones. "I am now much better able to leave my country and family, because I can so easily chat with whomever I want, all while I stay at home." This not only saves Sam time and jetlag, but also tremendous expense.

Many organizations like Sam's are thinking and acting globally as a way to extend their mission and impact. Because of the many technologies that allow international movements to flourish, the pendulum is swinging more and more toward global interconnectedness. That brings many opportunities to change the world, but it also can bring misunderstandings, as our world's many cultures are now in much closer proximity.

Each of us brings to the table our own unique set of values and cultural identities, some of which may clash or be inconsistent with those of the communities in which we work. I (Jeffrey) frequently find myself confused and at odds with what is going on around me, trying to reconcile my good intentions with the actual effects of my actions, as they are perceived by those I am trying to help. Ultimately, the "customer" is always right, in the sense that if they don't appreciate our efforts, or if we are operating with cultural insensitivity, we can do more harm than good. You may have experienced that phenomenon personally, as a client whose service call was forwarded to India or elsewhere, when you became aware that communication issues were getting in the way.

With a new, smaller, more interconnected world, there are certainly challenges that exist, but opportunities for social change are almost limitless. Potential is not the issue anymore. Anyone with a desire to help, and the means to make the journey can greatly impact their own corner of the world. The issue then becomes which corner of the world to impact, and in what way?

FIND YOUR NICHE

As the world continues to consolidate, megacompanies merge and consolidate just as European countries have aligned themselves in a union. This consolidation effort may make it appear as if you'll have to carve out your own special niche from a much tougher landscape. After all, what could you possibly offer that hasn't been done before? If the world is becoming so small, doesn't that mean there is less room for you to make your mark?

Even though we (Jeffrey and Mike) are of different generations, we each grew up thinking that whatever we might want to do has probably already been done. This has been a trend since the beginning of time; every generation believes that any revolutionary idea or advancement has been thought of by someone else. As a student many decades ago, I (Jeffrey) remember struggling to think of a research topic that could be fresh when it struck me that everything useful in my field had already been discovered. It was the same thing with writing my first book (about ethics) in which I wondered what I could possibly contribute that might be fresh. I remember feeling despondent that I was born too late to contribute anything meaningful to my field; it had all been done before.

As many of you just begin new careers, and new stages of life, you might also wonder what you might contribute that is useful and significant. Here's the good news: with most big organizations trying to handle massive projects on a large scale, they lose a certain flexibility and responsiveness. They have huge payrolls, elaborate and complex systems, and expensive operations (some companies' operating expenses are as high as 80 percent of their revenue). They can't function in nimble ways because they have so many rules, traditions, and people involved in making decisions.

Just think about the power of one. Consider what one person can do to make a difference when you don't have to answer to governing boards and community advisory boards, when you don't have to consult with a dozen different supervisors and colleagues before you take any kind of constructive action. Such oversight and collaboration are actually very important—we are not by any means suggesting that you function like a lone wolf doing whatever you want without adequate guidance and supervision. But what we are suggesting, just like that which was embodied in the stories throughout this book, is that you can do an incredible amount of important socially conscious work if you can find a niche and access your passion. Another key ingredient, also an important part of the stories, is how the leaders went out and got the training and education they needed to make their visions a reality.

A good mental exercise is to visualize swimming in a lazy current river that has a bunch of huge boulders spread throughout. There are rapids in certain sections, even waterfalls that must be negotiated, but most of the river flows at a slow pace. As you swim—or float—along the river, the boulders get bigger and bigger, yet you notice something else in the placement of them: the bigger the rocks, the more open spaces there are between them, easy for you to slip through. These spaces create even more room for independent, resourceful thinkers like yourself.

As the world becomes more polarized, what people often miss is the other end of the spectrum—the world of independents, free agents, and small movement builders who are living in these widening cracks and truly changing the world.

You remember the story of Dr. Kyra Bobinet, who started Vision Youthz. She saw a great need because there were no existing programs in place to help young inmates who were being released become assimilated to the real world or develop practical life skills that would help them to flourish in the outside world. They didn't know how to present themselves to prospective employers or how to pay bills or manage their money. This was clearly a big problem that had slipped between the rocks, so to speak. Although Kyra had no prior experience in starting a nonprofit, she launched a project to meet the needs she perceived.

If we made it seem like Kyra, Sam, or Blake's efforts were spun out of dreams, put into action and immediately successful, then we didn't adequately describe their disappointments, frustrations, and failures. Just as you would expect with anyone who is inadequately prepared for a job, each of us made many stupid blunders, critical errors, and miscalculations. The important lesson here is that we didn't give up, but instead learned from our mistakes and made needed adjustments. It takes more than motivation and commitment to make a difference—it also requires resilience and a certain stubbornness to keep going.

An Idea Born in the School Cafeteria

I'm from southern Texas, and in my high school there are a bunch of kids who can't even afford to eat lunch at the cafeteria. Lots of the kids have vouchers from the government that help pay for some of their lunch, but it's not that much money and it's clear that the kids who have these vouchers are not eating as much as my friends and me. The other day I was in line next to one of these kids and I ordered an ice cream with the rest of my food. I could just tell by the way he was looking at me that he would have loved to have an ice cream too. I started to think "why am I so special?" Then this idea clicked inside of me. What if I could get some of the kids in my school to donate part of their lunch money each month to other kids who can't afford it? If 200 of us donated just $50 each, that would be $1,000, which would be enough for 1,000 ice creams! I've started raising the money—some of the parents have been a little resistant, but most of my friends are really into it.

Within Farajii Muhammad's organization to help inner city youth in Baltimore, he began with a very clear sense of what he wanted to do. He had a clear niche and purpose that he could define and articulate. His ability to grow his project was directly related to keeping his focus at the forefront and not allowing himself to become distracted by other things. "There are a lot of needs that those big institutions don't cover, or don't address, *because* they are so big. We didn't want to be a one-stop shop for young people. We wanted to be a niche—leadership development for youth. We don't do issues like AIDS or homelessness. We didn't want to be all of that, because then our leadership programs would not have the high quality that we want."

Our own project in Nepal has remained tightly focused on a niche that had slipped between the boulders in the river. There are people asking all the time for money to build libraries and schools, to fund college scholarships abroad, to support colleges, to provide food and housing for their desperate needs.

Any successful enterprise must harness the resources and contributions of the local community. Unless you have the support of the elders and power brokers within the area in which you are operating, many of your efforts will be sabotaged or neglected. Any helping effort must represent a collaboration between outside assistance and local community leaders.

Yet we remain steadfast that we have one mission that we do very well, one that few others were addressing, so we focus on that goal and try to expand thoughtfully and efficiently.

Likewise, Elizabeth Hausler, the founder of Build Change, has found that focusing on her niche has not only helped her to identify what is important, but also what is *not* important. Defining that niche is almost like a guiding light for her, highlighting which organizational decisions are right for her to make: "Sticking to our mission—building earthquake resistant houses in the developing world—let us know what to do, and what not to do. We don't just take someone's donation or foundation money because it's there. If the funds are for building houses in New Orleans, that is a great mission, but it is not *our* mission. It's important for us to be consistent about what we do and that means turning down opportunities if they don't fit within that."

Finding a focused area to build within, and staying committed to that area, can elicit great impact. You don't always have to be all things to all people, and if your aim is too broad, chances are there is already somebody out there doing it anyway. The beautiful thing about finding a niche is that you can narrow it to the point at which you are one of the only contributors within that space, addressing a need that would otherwise have been ignored.

FOLLOW YOUR PASSION

If you want to leverage technology, focus on a niche need, and make a difference in the world, how do you know which project is the right one for you? If you don't find something that absolutely commands your interest and enthusiasm, you will find it difficult to stick with the project for very long. And sometimes, the worst thing you can do is to start something, get people's hopes up, and then not follow through. Such an uncompleted (though well intended) effort may very well make it impossible for anyone else to pick up the pieces that you left behind, because there was a breach of trust.

Of all the paths you choose, you may as well discover/find/choose something that resonates with who you are as an individual. And when you showcase that passion and take a stand for what you believe, you'll find that others will rally to support you. You'll recall in Matthew Flannery's story (Kiva) that he fumbled around for awhile before he settled on a path he was truly passionate about. But when he made the decision to focus on it, people stepped up to help bring that vision to life.

Coming out of college, Matthew wanted to be an entrepreneur, but all of his ideas for business were not things he was truly passionate about. They were things he thought would make him a lot of money. "I tried to start a DVD vending machine company, an online clothing company, an Internet toy company, but all of my ideas fizzled out because I didn't really care about them. Before I started Kiva, I was a failed entrepreneur in so many ways. I learned that your ideas will fizzle out if you really don't care about them. After nine months of working on Kiva, my friends were saying, 'Wow, you're still doing this!' And I knew inside myself that I was on to something."

Similar to Matthew, Jessica Mayberry identified something she was passionate about, film, and then found a way to promote change with that passion. After abandoning her television career, she still had a passion for film, as well as doing something with her skills that might be useful to people. One of her favorite quotes is from clergyman and community activist Howard Thurman, who said, "Don't ask what the world needs, ask what makes you come alive and go do it, because what the world needs is people who have come alive."

Jessica recalled, "When I was in my early 20s, I felt there was so much I needed to learn about why some people in the West have so much, and others have so little. I thought about doing a master's [degree] in international relations. But one of my mentors made it clear to me that I should use the skills that I have, and the things I was already passionate about—in my case, journalism and media—and use that as the basis of finding out a way to craft a field in international development. I did find my own way."

Sometimes it's easy to become so focused on changing the world that you forget to start with something you're truly passionate about. How do you find balance between your personal interests and what the world needs most? It's easy to get overwhelmed with these questions, but Sam Goldman shared how he reconciled what he had to offer with what might be needed most. "There is always going to seem like there's something more important that is worth doing. People are dying of waterborne diseases and I'm working on energy solutions. Lately, I've stopped a lot of those questions and I'm just trying to set my mind to something that I'm excited about. I can't solve all the world's problems, but I can make a difference with what excites me."

Looking inside yourself and identifying your passion can be the beginning of your own journey. It doesn't matter if it changes the world a little bit less than somebody else's effort. If it's something you love, then you'll have much more success with it than if you try to produce something that you're not honestly excited about.

So the question remains: How do you identify what you care about most? This isn't as easy a question as it might seem. Most of the people we profiled followed a template that was set early in life. They were so busy accumulating credits, following their ambitions, getting through daily life, that they didn't really know what they wanted to do. Many of them didn't figure out what they cared most about until they were already well out of school and working in their jobs.

Our own life stories parallel this pattern. Mike stumbled onto Roadtrip Nation because he felt so lost and aimless after graduating from college, no longer interested in going to medical school. He didn't realize that mentoring other college students would become his passion and calling until he found himself doing it and liked it. In other words, experimentation is a key: try different things until you discover something that moves your heart and soul. Fair warning: very few people are ever privileged enough to find work that is not only personally sustaining in the beginning, but remains so throughout their careers. Most people become burned out with what they do, but just keep doing it because they don't feel like they have other choices—which really means they don't want to take more risks.

Jeffrey also graduated college with no real direction or passion, so he went on to graduate school and started traveling. Jeffrey has had to reinvent himself almost every decade as a way to keep his passion flowing. It took 30 years of experimentation and life experience before he felt ready for the stage he's currently in, leading the project in Nepal. Every few years, he hears another calling and then decides whether he's still got the gumption to answer it.

IGNORE THE NAYSAYERS

It is all very important to solicit feedback and input from experts and consult with those who are far more experienced than you are. There is nothing that dooms a helping effort more than naïveté, inexperience, or ignorance about the nature of the problems and how they might be best addressed.

Even though supportive people are attracted to individuals following their own path, and want to offer their help, there will always be people who will try to knock you down. For one thing, being independent and forging your own road runs against the grain when compared to many of our cultural norms. For example, being part of a large company or other organizational entity is often seen as a badge of acceptance. General Electric, AmeriCorps, or other huge associations have their value in the world, but if they don't align with what it is you're passionate about, don't be afraid to go your own way.

Sometimes this kind of pressure to join the masses comes from the most unexpected places. We mentioned previously how Ariane Kirtley, founder of Amman Imman, had been warned in graduate school to never, ever try to do anything on your own but always work as part of an organized entity already in place. She tried international aid agencies first, but they all turned her down, saying her plan was impractical or not part of their mandate. It's a good thing she didn't succumb to all that pressure, or a half-million nomadic people in Northern Niger would still not have access to water.

MAINTAINING AUTHENTICITY

One of the values of going small and really focusing on a niche is that it's easier to maintain a sense of control and authenticity related to whatever you are trying to build. Within large organizations, where there are hundreds or thousands of people carrying out the objectives, it's often hard to maintain the sense of original purpose behind the effort. Also, as the size of the organization increases, so does the overhead to operate it, taking critical funds away from the need you are trying to service in the first place.

When we first established the Madhav Ghimire Foundation, we wanted to avoid the traps that are part of most other organizations. Perhaps because we have so little money in the first place, it was important to exert control and oversight to cover every dollar (or rupee) spent. We didn't want any paid staff or to waste money on offices or overhead. We also wanted to stay modest enough in size that we could continue to maintain active relationships with every one of our children and their families. The education we were providing would not be enough to sustain the girls unless they also had appropriate mentoring.

Many of the traditional organizational models currently in use are based on the need to support large structural entities with elaborate and complex systems. But if you're small, nimble, and smart, you can create your own organizational paradigm based on what is most relevant for your own focus.

As Matthew Flannery from Kiva shares, "If you had 10 million dollars, you probably wouldn't create our organizational chart, but it's very organic and it works for us. It's basically a web of friends and associations who have all gone through the fires together, so we have a lot of trust that was built through those hard times."

In addition to building a strong culture, keeping your organization small also leads to less bureaucracy. Aaron Bartley, founder of PUSH Buffalo, has worked for big unions and other institutions. "An advantage of staying small is that you're not bureaucratic. All the things you have to deal with in a big organization; all the general processes, the lack of ability to adjust quickly, making decisions quickly, or getting a message out. Ten different layers of management may affect a message before it ever gets out the door. Now I don't have to check with anybody before calling a reporter and sharing a message. Or deal with any other political realities."

By having less bureaucracy involved in the change you're trying elicit, you can more easily maintain the authenticity of the mission you started with. Going bigger may give you larger reach, but if that scale dilutes the ethos you started with, what is the point of all that scale at the end of the day?

STARTING LOCAL

There are so many adventurous stories of people flying all over the world to create change for those in need. But sometimes the best place to start is in your own backyard. Farajii Muhammad has taken "going local" to heart. As you read in Chapter 13, his New Light Leadership Coalition is fostering a new generation of youth leaders in the greater Baltimore area. He has expanded to surrounding communities around the mid-Atlantic region, but retains his core focus on his hometown. "Most of the time, when you think of great movements, you think those all began on a national level. But great movements like the civil rights movement, they all started small. Locally. Dr. King said if you organize locally, the power of that action will be so powerful that it will spread to a national level. What we saw in the civil rights movement in Birmingham was a local action that manifested itself to becoming a national action. So, organize locally. Don't worry about the national stuff. Just work right where you are, and then if it's powerful and influential enough, it will spread."

Farajii also points out that before you can be ready to change some part of the world, you first have to focus on changing yourself. "The first leader is the leader of self."

COLLABORATE

Much of the power associated with going small is when a large number of people collectively come together and synergize their efforts to create a highly effective, personal impact on a truly global scale. To do that, each person involved must learn how to collaborate and to think of him or herself as just one part of a much larger ecosystem. Elizabeth Hausler operates Build Change with this collective, modern approach: "You can't do it all on your own because sometimes you don't have enough resources. So sometimes we work with microfinance institutions like Kiva, whose niche can bring in those resources. And other times we'll work with local organizations where we're building houses, like in Indonesia where we only have 14 staff members who can provide us with local volunteers to help build the houses. Learning how to partner and leverage other people's specialized skills is really important for what we do and for long-term change."

Collaborating with lots of different types of organizations also means that Elizabeth has to be fluid and adaptable, to the operating styles and cultures of those organizations. "I have to be a bit of a chameleon and play different roles to get all these partnerships going. One day I'm meeting with this completely grassroots organization that can provide us with volunteers, so I'll wear sandals and a t-shirt. And then the next day I'll be meeting with The American Red Cross, where I have to get all dressed up and have this very official, conservative meeting."

And how does Elizabeth even know when a partnership is a good fit for her effort? "The biggest indicator is if it is a good philosophical alignment. Anyone we partner with has to care about earthquake-resistant houses. If the organization you're partnering with has objectives that differ too much, then the partnership won't work."

For Austin Gutwein, the 13-year-old founder of Hoops of Hope, creating partnerships was a huge part of getting his effort off the ground, especially since he was only nine years old when he started. Right off the bat, he partnered with World Vision to help give him an outlet for the funds he would raise. That way, Austin could just focus on what he loved to do, shooting free throws with as many kids as possible to raise the money and then letting World Vision take it from there.

Regrets on My Deathbed

I'm 75 years old. I have 14 grandkids and 5 children. My family is beautiful, and they're the most important thing in my life. But getting older is a funny thing. You start to be less scared of things because you've already lived such a long life. The one thing that I have yet to do is leave this country and try to do some international service work. I've always wanted to do it, but for one reason or another I always found an excuse not to go out there. Now I realize I only have a little time left on this planet, and I want to get out there and do it. What's holding me back? My age? I've been waiting my whole life to do something like this. If I was on my deathbed this would be the one thing I would have regretted not doing, so you better bet that I'm not going to let anything get in my way.

DO SOMETHING

An organization that is "alive" and organic grows and evolves in response to input from its members as well as the constituents who are being helped. It is inevitable that where you end up will not be exactly where you thought you would be from the outset. It's easy to sit around forever, continuing to hone and perfect your skills and plan, but in the end you just have to get out there and start the process.

The project that formed the nucleus for this book looks very different now than it did when we began writing about it a year ago. We received feedback and suggestions from the children and their families, as well as the teachers in the schools, which guided us to become more responsive to their needs. Students and team members who participated in our visits offered other input about ways we might become more effective in our efforts. Any time someone made a suggestion, "Why don't you try this?" or "Have you thought of that?" our response would be, "Great idea! Why don't you get that going?"

A truly grassroots organization is one in which everyone involved "owns" the entity, has a voice in its development, and feels the freedom to work according to individual interests as well as client needs. One person returned from Nepal to start a book donation drive, building libraries in the schools by collecting children's books from parents. She also raised money to pay for postage to ship the books abroad. Another person focused on technology needs, exploring ways to provide Internet access and laptops for teachers and children in rural areas where such resources are unknown. Another team member realized that village teachers had very little training in their craft and so organized workshops for districts in cooperative learning strategies. Another arranged for children in elementary schools in the United States to begin pen pal communications with counterparts in Nepal. Someone initiated marketing activities to print posters and brochures to help promote the fundraising efforts. Two volunteers, young students from Europe, agreed to spend a year in one of the villages, tutoring the scholarship girls in their English proficiency. Two other students returned to begin fundraising efforts to provide more scholarships for needy children.

The list goes on and on. It is most amazing that all of these new innovations took place in the last year alone! And many of these developments were things that we could have never predicted had we not initiated the process in the first place. In fact, if we had waited until we perfected the plan, we might have never even started the journey.

How You Can Put Your Hopes and Dreams into Action

Intention is one thing; action is quite another. This practical section reviews some of the different options and opportunities that are available to students and young professionals to make a difference in the world or in their own communities. There are so many different causes and projects that you might become involved with, depending on your interests and passion. Just a few of the most important areas include the following.

- *Reproductive and child health.* You might find it surprising that of all the causes of death among women in developing countries, childbirth is number one.

1 in 60 pregnant women die, compared to 1 in 3,000 in the west. Furthermore, two-thirds of infants and children who die could have been saved if only they had the most basic health care.

- *Education.* Two-thirds of women and girls in the world are illiterate with limited access to education.
- *Infectious diseases.* Malaria, for one, kills a *half-billion* people each year, most of them young children. Tuberculosis is another preventable killer that strikes the young.

This girl from the Kayan tribe of northern Thailand is one of millions of children who are denied basic education and healthcare. There is no shortage of causes in which you can volunteer your efforts to help. The key is to find a cause about which you care deeply and can feel useful.

- *Water resources.* After oxygen, water is the most basic human need, yet most of the developing world lacks safe water supplies and sanitation.
- *Malnutrition.* Growth and lifespan are severely compromised by inadequate food supplies and poor diets.
- *Human rights.* Religious and personal freedom are curtailed in many areas of the world, where people are subjected to persecution, oppression, or death if they subscribe to beliefs that are different from those of the ruling party.
- *Natural disasters.* Relief after floods, earthquakes, tsunamis, storms, mudslides, and droughts.

Whereas most people have heard of organizations such as the Peace Corp, AmeriCorps, and Habitat for Humanity, there are limitless other possibilities to consider. As just a few examples of the landscape:

- *Ambassadors for Children* (www.ambassadorsforchildren.org) provides volunteers with opportunities to work with disadvantaged children in Latin America, Eastern Europe, and Asia, as well as on native American reservations.
- *WorldTeach* (www.worldteach.org) supplies volunteer teachers in developing countries during the summer. You live with a host family in Africa, Asia, or South America and teach English and/or an area of expertise.
- *Global Volunteers* (www.globalvolunteers.org) is committed to working in cooperation with local needs throughout the world. Volunteers teach English, help build schools, work with at-risk children, or assist in community development.
- *Cross-Cultural Solutions* (www.crossculturalsolutions.org) places volunteers in orphanages, schools, health facilities, and community centers, working in areas of interest and greatest need.

This is just the briefest sampling of options among the hundreds that are available. However, as we have demonstrated in this book, it isn't necessary to even be part of an organization to work toward social justice issues. The important thing is just to begin the journey, and open yourself to the experiences you're about to have. In the end, it doesn't matter *what* you do, as long as you do *something.*

References and Resources

Andreasen, S. (2007). Social inclusion and local democracy. *MS Nepal Magazine*. Retrieved March, 2008 from http://www.ms.dk/sw69602.asp.

Asher, S. J., Huffaker, G. Q., & McNally, M. (1994). Therapeutic considerations of wilderness experiences for incest and rape survivors. *Women and Therapy, 15,* 161–174.

Ausenda, F., & McCloskey, E. (2006). *World volunteers: The world guide to humanitarian and development volunteering.* New York: Universe.

Barber, N. (2004). *Kindness in a cruel world: The evolution of altruism.* Amherst, NY: Prometheus.

Beck, J. (2005). *Cognitive therapy for challenging problems: What to do when the basics don't work.* New York: Guilford.

Boyle, D. P., Nackerud, L., & Kilpatrick, A. (1999). The road less traveled: Cross-cultural, international experiential learning. *International Social Work, 42*(2), 201–214.

Brice, R. (2008). King of the hill. *Outside,* March, 120–122.

Broad, S. (2003). Living the Thai life: A case study of volunteer tourism at the Gibbon Rehabilitation Project. *Tourism Recreation Research, 28*(3), 63–72.

Brown, S., & Lehto, X. (2005). Traveling with a purpose: Understanding the motives and benefits of volunteer vacationers. *Current Issues in Tourism, 8*(6), 479–496.

Brown, S., & Morrison, A. (2003). Expanding volunteer vacation participation: An exploratory study of the mini-mission concept. *Tourism Recreation Research, 28*(3), 73–82.

Busson, A. (2007). Hands-on philanthropy. *Newsweek*, May 28, E4.

Cahill, T. (1996). *Jaguars ripped my flesh*. New York: Vintage Books.

Curwin, T. (2007, May 7). Club mad. *Los Angeles Times*, p. L5.

Clary, E. G., Snyder, M., Ridge, R., Copeland, J., Stukas, A., Haugen, J., & Miene, P. (1998). Understanding and assessing the motivations of volunteers: A functional approach. *Journal of Personality and Social Psychology, 74*(6), 1516–1530.

Coghlan, A. (2006). Volunteer tourism as an emerging trend or an expansion of ecotourism? *International Journal of Nonprofit and Voluntary Sector Marketing, 11*(3), 225–238.

Collins, J., DeZerega, S., & Heckscher, Z. (2001). *How to live your dream of volunteering overseas*. New York: Penguin.

Dryden, W. (2008). *Rational emotive behavior therapy: Distinctive features*. New York: Routledge.

Dukes, R. L. (2006). Reflections on the meaning of a Semester at Sea voyage after 22 years. *Psychological Reports, 98*(1), 209–216.

Ellis, C., & Carlson, J. (2008). *Cross cultural awareness and social justice in counseling*. New York: Routledge.

Evans, D., Hearn, M., Uhlemann, M., & Ivey, A. (2007). *Essential interviewing: A programmed approach to effective communication*. Belmont, CA: Wadsworth.

Fedarko, K. (2007, July). High times. *Outside*, 93–111.

Ferruci, P. (2006). *The power of kindness: The unexpected benefits of leading a compassionate life*. New York: Tarcher.

Fitzpatrick, L. (2007). Does volunteer tourism do any good? *Time*, Aug. 6, 49–51.

Flora, C. (2008). Earth angels. *Psychology Today*, January/February, 45–46.

Fouad, N. A., Gerstein, L. H., & Toporek, R. L. (2006). Social justice and counseling psychology in context. In R. Toporek, L. Gerstein, N. Fouad, G. Roysircar, & T. Israel (Eds.), *Handbook of social justice in counseling psychology: Leadership, vision, and action*. Thousand Oaks, CA: Sage.

Gebhard, N., Marriner, M., & Gordon, J. (2003). *Roadtrip nation: A guide to discovering your path in life*. New York: Ballantine.

Gillis, H. L., & Simpson, C. (1991). Project choices: Adventure-based residential drug treatment for court-referred youth. *Journal of Addictions and Offender Counseling, 12*, 12–27.

Gould, J. L., & Marler, P. (1987, January). Learning by instinct. *Scientific American*, 74–85.

Hillary, E. (1964). *Schoolhouse in the clouds*. New York: Doubleday.

Ihle, E., Ritsher, J., & Kanas, N. (2006). Positive psychological outcomes of spaceflight: An empirical study. *Aviation, Space, and Environmental Medicine*, 77(2), 93–101.

Katz, R. (2007). Pop!Tech: Interview with Kiva's Jessica Flannery. Worldchanging. http://www.worldchanging.com/archives//007448.html. Accessed August, 2008.

Kennedy, C. (2007). Making a difference at home. *Time*, Sept. 10, 68.

Kottler, J. (2008). *A basic primer of helping skills*. Thousand Oaks, CA: Sage.

Kottler, J.A. (1997). *Travel that can change your life*. San Francisco: Jossey-Bass.

Kottler, J. A. (2000). *Doing good: Passion and commitment for helping others*. Philadelphia: Brunner/Routledge.

Kottler, J. A. (2001). *Making changes last*. Philadelphia: Brunner/Routledge.

Kottler, J. A., & Montgomery, M. (2000). Prescriptive travel and adventure-based activities as an adjunct to counselling. *Guidance and Counselling*, 15(2), 8–11.

Lee, C., & Hipolito-Delgado, C. (2007). Counselors as agents of social justice. In C. Lee (Ed.), *Counseling for social justice* (2nd ed.). Alexandria, VA: American Counseling Association.

Little, D. E., & Schmidt, C. (2006). Self, wonder, and God! The spiritual dimensions of travel experiences. *Tourism*, 54(2), 107–116.

Lum, D. (2007). *Culturally competent practice: A framework for understanding diverse groups and justice issues* (3rd ed.). Belmont, CA: Thomson.

Marriner, M., McAllister, B., Gebhard, N., & Bollinger, R. (2005). *Finding the open road: A guide to self-construction rather than mass production*. Berkeley, CA: Ten Speed Press.

McMillon, B., Cutchins, D., & Geissinger, A. (2006). *Volunteer vacations: Short-term adventures that will benefit you and others*. Chicago: Chicago Review Press.

McNeil, D. G. (2007). Sex slaves returning home raise AIDS risks, study says. *New York Times International*, Aug. 1, A7.

Miner, J., & Boldt, J. (2002). *Outward Bound USA: Crew not passengers*. Seattle: Mountaineers Books.

Minichiello, V., & Kottler, J. (Eds.) (2009). *Qualitative journeys: Student and mentor experiences with research*. Thousand Oaks, CA: Sage.

Mortenson, G., & Relin, D. (2006). *Three cups of tea*. New York: Penguin.

Nepal Ministry of Health (1998). *Family health survey*. Kathmandu, Nepal.

Nielsen, L. W. (2007). Yes madam. *MS Nepal Magazine*. Retrieved March, 2008. http://www.msnepal.org/stories_articles/miscellaneous/yesmadam.htm.

Nordfalk, A. M. (2007). Democracy can only be created in interaction with the people. *MS Nepal Magazine*, #1. Retrieved March, 2008 from http://www.ms.dk/sw69613.asp.

Oman, D. (2007). Does volunteering foster physical health and longevity? In S. G. Post (Ed.), *Altruism and health: Perspectives from empirical research*. New York: Oxford University Press, 15–32.

Pandey, N. (2002). Charting out a vision for the future. *The Rising Nepal*, March 23, *10*.

Post, S. G. (Ed.) (2007). *Altruism and health: Perspectives from empirical research*. New York: Oxford University Press.

Post, S. G. (2005). Altruism, happiness, and health: It's good to be good. *International Journal of Behavioral Medicine, 12*(2), 66–77.

Rapoport, R., & Castenera, M. (1994). *I should have stayed home: The worst trips of great writers*. Berkeley: Book Passage Press.

Regmi, K., & Kottler, J. (2009). An epidemiologist learns grounded theory. In V. Minichiello & J. Kottler (Eds.), *Qualitative journeys: Student and mentor experiences with research*. Thousand Oaks, CA: Sage.

Ryder, J. A. (2006). College student volunteerism: A quantitative analysis of psychological benefits gained through time spent in service to others. *Dissertation Abstracts, 66*(8-A), 2845.

Sachs, J. D. (2007). A global coalition of good. *Time*, Sept. 17, p. 49.

Schmidt, B. C. (2000). The service sojourn: Conceptualizing the college student volunteer experience. *Dissertation Abstracts International, 61*(2A) 499.

Schwartz, C. (2007). Altruism and subjective well-being: Conceptual models and empirical support. In S. G. Post (Ed.), *Altruism and health: Perspectives from empirical research*. New York: Oxford University Press, 33–42.

Scott, N., & Seglow, J. (2008). *Altruism*. United Kingdom: Open University Press.

Sherman, P. W. (1980). The meaning of nepotism. *American Naturalist, 116*, 604–606.

Silverman, J., Decker, M., Gupta, J., & Maheshwari, A. (2006). HIV prevalence and predictors among rescued sex trafficked women and girls in Mumbai, India. *Journal of Acquired Immune Deficiency Syndromes, 43*(5), 588–593.

Stebbins, R. A., & Graham, M. (2004). *Volunteering as leisure, leisure as volunteering: An international assessment*. Oxon: CABI.

Stengel, R. (2007). A time to serve. *Time*, Sept. 10, 50–55.

Theroux, P. (1992). *The happy isles of Oceania*. New York: Ballantine.

Thoits, P. A., & Hewitt, L. N. (2001). Volunteer work and well-being. *Journal of Health and Social Behavior, 42*, 115–131.

Ungar, M. (2003). Lessons on "otherness": What therapists can learn from traveling. *Journal of Systemic Therapies, 22*(4), 1–14.

Vera, E. M., & Speight, S. L. (2007). Advocacy, outreach, and prevention: Integrating social action roles in professional training. In E. Aldarondo (Ed.), *Advancing social justice through clinical practice*. Mahwah, NJ: Lawrence Erlbaum.

Wearing, S. L. (2001). *Volunteer tourism: Seeking experiences that make a difference*. Wallingford: CABI.

Wilding, C., & Milne, A. (2008). *Teach yourself cognitive therapy*. New York: McGraw-Hill.

Wilson, E., & Harris, C. (2006). Meaningful travel: Women, independent travel and the search for self and meaning. *Tourism, 54*(2), 161–172.

Winerman, L. (2006). Helping others, helping ourselves. *Monitor on Psychology, 37*(11), 38.

Zahra, A. (2006). The unexpected road to spirituality via volunteer tourism. *Tourism, 54*(2), 173–185.

About the Authors

Jeffrey A. Kottler is one of the most prolific authors in the helping professions, having written over 7 books about a wide range of subjects. He has authored a dozen texts for counselors and therapists that are used in universities around the world and a dozen books each for practicing therapists and educators. Some of his most highly regarded works include: *On Being a Therapist, The Imperfect Therapist, Compassionate Therapy, The Mummy at the Dining Room Table, Bad Therapy, The Client Who Changed Me*, and *Making Changes Last*. He has also authored several books for the public that describe rather complex phenomena in highly accessible prose: *Travel That Can Change Your Life, Private Moments, Secret Selves, The Language of Tears, The Last Victim: Inside the Minds of Serial Killers*, and *Divine Madness: Ten Stories of Creative Struggle*.

Jeffrey has been an educator for 30 years. He has worked as a teacher, counselor, and therapist in preschool, middle school, mental health center, crisis center, university, community college, and private practice settings. He has served as a Fulbright Scholar and Senior Lecturer in Peru (1980) and Iceland (2000) and worked as a Visiting Professor in New Zealand, Australia, Hong Kong, Singapore, and Nepal. Jeffrey is currently Professor of Counseling at California State University, Fullerton. He also established the Madhav Ghimire Foundation, which is devoted to helping the most neglected children of Nepal.

Mike Marriner is the co-founder of Roadtrip Nation, a grassroots organization that mobilizes students to hit the road, interview leaders from all walks of life, and explore the world for themselves. Footage from these trips is shared with individuals everywhere through the *Roadtrip Nation* series on PBS, published books, various broadcast partnerships, and online at www.roadtripnation.com.

Mike graduated from Pepperdine University with degrees in biology and kinesiology and a NCAA Division I water polo national championship. After graduation, he felt sheltered and underexposed to the world around him. He hit the road with two friends in an unsound 1985 green RV to interview people who defined their own roads in life, including the founder of Starbucks, lobstermen, artists, the founder of Barnes and Noble, the CEO of National Geographic Ventures, the scientist who decoded the human genome, the CEO of Dell Computers, truck drivers, filmmakers, social activists, and many others. This road trip not only changed their lives, but spawned a whole social movement that has developed partnerships with more than 50 universities in North America.

Mike has co-authored three previous books, including *Roadtrip Nation: A Guide to Discovering Your Path in Life*, which reached #15 on the Amazon.com rankings and #1 on the Barnesandnoble.com business rankings. He has also co-produced the annual *Roadtrip Nation* television series, which airs nationally on PBS, and has been featured on NBC's *Today Show*, NBC's *Carson Daly Show*, CBS's *Early Show*, CNN, CNBC, *CBS News*, *BBC World News*, NPR, and many other broadcast outlets. He has also been listed on *Esquire*'s "Best and Brightest Genius List," and featured in magazines such as *Newsweek, Outside, Forbes, Teen People, Fast Company, Anthem, Flaunt*, and many others. He has presented to audiences from Oxford University in England to major corporations such as Hewlett Packard, Starbucks, Merck, State Farm, and others.

About the DVD

Introduction

This appendix provides you with information on the contents of the DVD that accompanies this book.

DVD Help

Tips for Playing the DVD

You can play this DVD using your computer's DVD drive or the DVD player connected to your television. The DVD should start automatically when you place it in your DVD drive or player.

- **On a PC running Windows XP or Vista:** If you have more than one media player installed on your computer, Windows may ask you to choose one to play the DVD. After you do, the DVD should start in that media player and play the Introduction.

  To navigate through the DVD, use your mouse to select from the menu system instead of using your media player's navigation pane. Depending on the media player you choose, you may need to click once to select a menu item and click again to play it.
- **On a Macintosh running Mac OS X:** The DVD should start in the default media player and play the Introduction.

To navigate through the DVD, use your mouse to select from the menu system instead of using your media player's navigation pane. Depending on the media player you choose, you may need to click once to select a menu item and click again to play it.

- **On a DVD player connected to your television:** After the Introduction, use your player's remote control to navigate through the DVD's menu system.

What's on the DVD

This DVD is intended to inspire you further through the stories of students, educators, and professionals who are featured in the text. You will see and hear team members struggle with various challenges along the way, as well as speak from their hearts about what they are experiencing. Regardless of their age and life experience, participants talk about how being involved in a service project has impacted their future goals and aspirations.

Each of the three sections of the DVD consist of vignettes that show scenic footage, visits to villages, and interviews with those who participated in our project. You will join the team on their journey and then hear their reflections on what they learned and how they were transformed, after which we discuss some of the themes that emerged that are most relevant to the content of the book.

Customer Care

If you have trouble with the DVD-ROM, please call the Wiley Product Technical Support phone number at (800) 762-2974. Outside the United States, call 1(317) 572-3994. You can also contact Wiley Product Technical Support at http://support.wiley.com. John Wiley & Sons will provide technical support only for installation and other general quality control items. For technical support on the applications themselves, consult the program's vendor or author.

To place additional orders or to request information about other Wiley products, please call (877) 762-2974.